The complete collection

EFC KITS

Royal Blue, Salmon Pink. A journey from 1878 to present.

WRITTEN AND COMPILED BY JAMES CLEARY

Sport Media
A Trinity Mirror Business

ACKNOWLEDGEMENTS

With thanks to all those who have helped with material, be it text or images for this project. Special thanks go to Karen Sayers and Max Dunbar at the Liverpool Record Office, who helped unveil some useful information, by kind permission of the Everton Collection Charitable Trust. Likewise credit must go for use of images, particularly from early years. Thanks to Glen Hind and the Collins's , for use of original shirts, and Gavin Buckland for statistics and facts. The historical kits website was an invaluable resource in confirming or disputing some of my picture research, while credit should also go to John Devlin's True Colours, which provided an extra resource for later strips. And to Barry Parker for his design work, despite his allegiance.

Sport Media
A Trinity Mirror Business

Published in Great Britain in 2009 by:

Trinity Mirror Sport Media,

PO Box 48, Old Hall Street,

Liverpool L69 3EB

Executive Editor: KEN ROGERS

Art Editor: RICK COOKE

Designer: BARRY PARKER

ISBN 978-1906-80231-8 : Printed and finished by Korotan

INTRODUCTION

From humble origins, formed as St Domingo's in 1878 via Stanley Park, Priory Road, Anfield and currently Goodison Park for near 120 years, Everton FC have enjoyed a long and distinguised history. Founder members of the Football League and Premier League, the club are readily identified by their traditional strip of royal blue shirts, white shorts and socks. Club kits, arguably more than any other factor, are representative of a club's origins, influences, often relationship with neighbouring sides or ones further afield. Much credited but worth emphasising, Juventus owe their black and white striped colours to Notts County, the oldest professional club in the world. The story went that sometime in the early 20th century, needing to replace their fading pink shirts, they asked their English player John Savage if he had any contacts in his home country who could supply new shirts in colours more suited to the elements. He had a friend who lived in Nottingham, and thus being a fan of the Magpies, shipped out shirts in the colours of his side — and the rest is history.

Such tales are common in the emergence of colours

inextricably linked to a team — and Everton are no exception. Of course, the club weren't always known for their blue and white colours — as can be discovered inside. It seemed an opportune time then to celebrate the club's progress both on and off the pitch for over 130 years. There is a new kit deal with sportswear manufacturer Le Coq Sportif, whose previous relationship with Everton heralded the greatest season in the club's history — 1984-85, a factor celebrated in the design of the new home strip (pictured), an updated tribute to that famous shirt. This book is as comprehensive as we could factor. Examples of new strips, new colours used in one-off games continue to come to light, but we have tried to portray and note as many home and away strips, plus goalkeeping colours as possible. We have also used original shirts, logos, badges and other kit notables — plus an additional miscellaneous section including some classic fashions and advertisements. We have aimed to follow the development of the game by virtue of the more regular change in strips and fashions, reflected in the commercialisation of the game from the late 1970s. I hope it will meet your approval.

James Cleary

CONTENTS

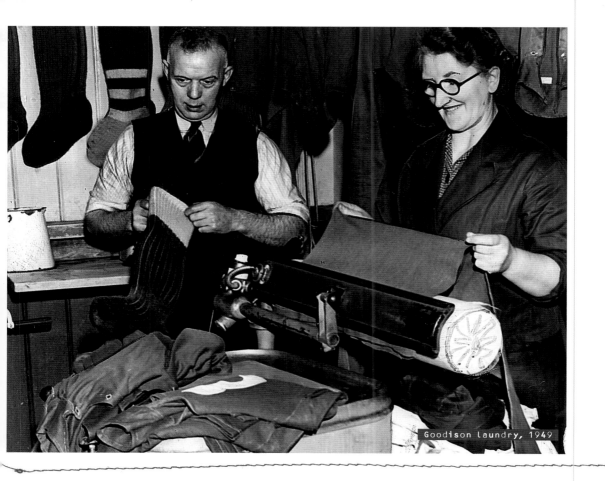

Goodison laundry, 1949

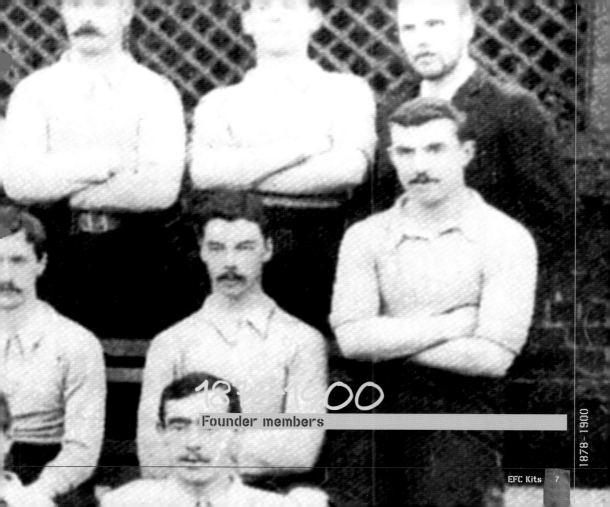

1878-1900
Founder members

1878-1900

ABOUT THE KIT

There is confusion over the earliest incarnation of Everton strips. As was common, new players would play in the shirts of their old team. To prevent this, the secretary would apparently dye the shirts black, and have a two-inch scarlet sash sewn in. This led to the nickname "Black Watch", after the army regiment. Access to ledgers in the Everton Collection reveals the following information from the early years of the club's Football League days. The club planned to play in 'salmon coloured shirts with dark maroon pants' ahead of 1890-91; this idea was ammended six weeks later to 'blue knickers'. Shirts, rather than 'jerseys' were to be used in the middle of that season: 'Order 30 salmon shirts and 12 Blue and Gold...'. Red shirts with blue trimmings were to be adopted for the 1891-92 season (right), the club's last at Anfield. And that

'Cambridge Blue' colours be adopted for 1892-93, the first season at Goodison. This new evidence raises doubt upon the salmon pink and navy blue away strip launched in 1992 by Umbro, a 100-year tribute to what was apparently Everton's first kit at L4 4EL. Other pictorial evidence comes from sketches. An 1890 game at Blackburn shows dark shirts, white shorts and half dark/white socks. An 1892 FA Cup replay against Burnley is also inconclusive, although dark shorts and socks are visible. The following season, there is evidence to suggest blue shirts were worn at Goodison Park. Hosting Nottingham Forest, Everton, who at this stage wore red (or was it still salmon pink?), changed their shirts due to a colour clash. The Liverpool Mercury reported: 'Everton wore new jerseys and their deep blue colour made a distinct and pretty contrast

1883-84

1891

with the bright red of Forest.' The club's first FA Cup final, against Wolves, saw dark shirts, white 'baggies' and dark socks apparent. Reflections from the 1897 final, described Everton wearing light blue shirts and white shorts.

ON-FIELD

With the Football League being formed in 1888, Everton were one of the last teams to become one of 12 founder members. The club's greater facilities at Anfield appears to have been a key factor in acceptance, ahead of Bootle. Having finished as runners-up the previous season (also recording the club's record score, 11-2, against Derby in the FA Cup), 1890-91 saw Everton win their first league title, despite losing their last two games. An agonising 3-2 defeat at Burnley on the final day proved irrelevant as champions Preston, who would have made it three successive league crowns with a victory, went down 3-0 at Sunderland. Everton would also become the first team to be awarded a championship trophy (and medals for the players), Preston having only been awarded a pennant to recognise their two titles. The club also finish as runners-up in the FA Cup in 1893, losing 1-0 to Wolves at Fallowfield, Manchester. The 1894-95 season (they would finish runners-up) saw

1881 Home

Everton win the first Football League derby against Liverpool, winning 3-0 with Tom McInnes gaining the honour of netting the first goal. It was also the last of

OFF-FIELD

The first incarnation of the club was formed in 1878 by a group who attended St Domingo's Church School – who played at Stanley Park. St Domingo's became Everton in November 1879, playing their first game a month later.
The players' reward for winning the club's first Championship

a club record 12 successive wins, a sequence which had begun with four wins at the end of the previous season. 1897 saw another FA Cup final defeat, 3-2 to Aston Villa.

in 1890-91? A £5 bonus, plus a gold medal.
Penalty kicks were introduced for the 1891-92 campaign.
Kelly Bros were given the task to develop Goodison Park. They began work in 1892 on 7 June – it was declared ready by FA president Lord Kinnaird on 27 August.

EVERTON COLLECTION

The following excerpts are taken from official club ledgers. Thanks to the Everton Collection Charitable Trust:

1888-89
Saturday August 27 1888

Resolved that the ordering of outfit for players be left in the hands of the secretaries.

1890-91
Monday May 12 1890

Colours: It has [been] decided that the colours of the club for next season be salmon coloured shirts with dark maroon pants.

Monday June 23 1890

Colours: It was resolved that the colors (sic) for the ensuing season be salmon colored (sic) shirt with dark blue knickers.

Monday December 1 1890

Stocks (?): Resolved that we have shirts instead of jerseys in the future and that the secretary order 30 salmon shirts and 12 Blue and Gold...

1891-92
Monday June 15 1891

Club colours: Resolved that we adopt as colours for the new season red shirt with blue trimmings.

Monday June 22 1891

Resolved that we have dark blue knickers for next season.

1892-93
Monday May 9 1892

Club colours: Resolved that we register Cambridge Blue shirts...knickers as the club colours.

BOB 1878-1978

As the Bob Latchford cutting shows (right, taken from a late 70s football album), there were suggestions the first kit was a blue and white halved creation, with white shorts and socks.

UP THE ENGLISH

The 1-0 win for Wolves in the 1893 FA Cup final was well received in the press — their XI was made up of Englishmen.

Mid-1890s

BOB GOES BACK – 100 YEARS

EVERTON striker Bob Latchford (right) took a trip down memory lane last season to help celebrate the year 1878. That's when it all began for Everton—with a club named Stanley Park.

Bob tried out their first blue and white strip and commented: "They were tough lads in those days but I think they would get laughed off the park today."

NOVEMBER 1890

Kit evidence of the period can be gleaned from the local press during these years. According to a report in the Liverpool Mercury on 3 November 1890, 'Everton donned...dark-blue jerseys with white fronts — a transformation from the salmon tint certainly.' A month later, the same newspaper reported, 'Everton appeared in comfortable-looking dark jerseys of narrow blue and yellow stripes which contrasted strongly with those worn by Wolves which were of red and white tint.'

DID YOU KNOW?

September 1888 saw Everton beat Accrington Stanley 2-1 at Anfield in Merseyside's first Football League game — George Fleming scoring both goals.

Everton's 11,000+ average attendance in 1890-91 was the first time a five-figure average had been recorded. Fred Geary scored the first goal at Goodison Park, in a friendly against Bolton. He also scored Everton's first competitive goal there,

1889 Team

although the honour of first competitive goal went to Nottingham Forest's Horace Pike - the league game ended in a 2-2 draw.

Four Everton players were in England's XI in April 1891. Edgar Chadwick, Fred Geary, Johnny Holt and Alf Milward played against Scotland. This has happened in only three other games — Gary Stevens, Trevor Steven, Peter Reid and Gary Lineker all played three times at the 1986 World Cup.

1895 Keeper

1878-1900

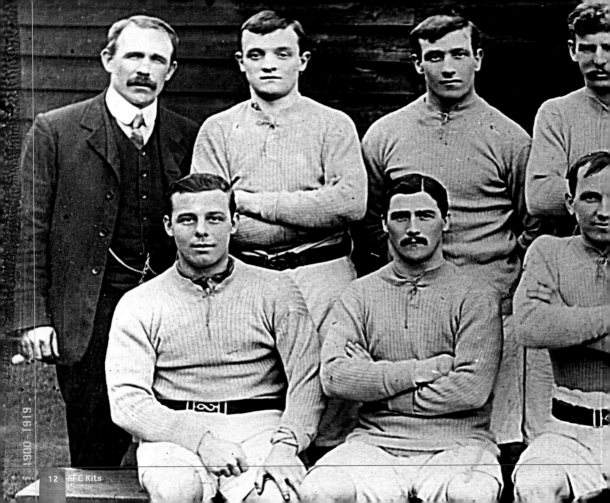

1900-1919
Cup first, champions at war

1900-1919

ABOUT THE KIT

The royal blue shirts became the norm in the early part of the 1900s. Regulations were also relaxed that had required players to cover their knees. Shorts ('knickerbockers' or 'knickers') became shorter, while for the first time socks ('stockings') became part of the official club strip. Initially self-coloured, these would soon incorporate contrasting rings on the turnover, for example. Generally the trend in the Football League, these would be dark, pale colours not becoming standard until the 1950s. Shirts with laced crew necks were common — Everton's being no exception — though a variety of collar designs were evident. Stripes would become popular, the trend being for wider stripes making the wearer, in theory, appear taller — while hoops (more common in both forms of rugby) would emphasise the wearer's bulk.

Pictures from the 1906 and 1907 FA Cup finals suggest the kit at this time consisted of baggy blue shirts, with white shorts and black socks — incorporating a blue trim on the turn-ups. In terms of the latter half of the period, 1910 and '11 cartoons suggest the Everton strip remained as blue shirts, white shorts and black socks. The 1914-15 title-winning side's shirt, apart from lace-up collar, differed little from the 1906 Cup winners. Black socks also incorporated white and blue hooped turn-ups.

1906-07 Home

1909 Team

ON-FIELD

It was a period of near misses — but also saw some tangible success. Jimmy Settle became the first Everton player to finish as top scorer in the League in 1901-02, the Blues finishing second — a position they achieved again in 04-05. The FA Cup was won for the first time in 1906. The scorer in the 1-0 win, Alex "Sandy" Young, also finished as the league's top scorer the following season when a third second-place finish in the 00s was again achieved. Bert Freeman hit 38 in 37 in his first full season at Everton, as the Blues finished runners-up in 08-09. This was a record goals total, standing until 1926. First Division runners-up in 11-12, the Blues

FA Cup final players, 1907

were champions three years later as the outbreak of the First World War was taking hold. They pipped Oldham, despite losing 11 of 38 games – finishing with the lowest

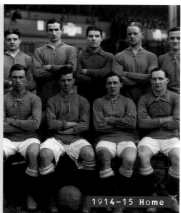
1914-15 Home

points per game average of any team winning the title. Bobby Parker would finish as the league's top scorer, before official action was suspended until 1919-20.

FA Cup final, 1906

OFF-FIELD

1907 saw the original Park End stand completed, a structure that remained until January 1994 — when a standing terrace was last used at Goodison in the FA Cup third-round replay against Bolton. The Archibald Leitch-designed Main Stand was completed in 1909, remaining a notable Goodison landmark until the late 1960s. The triple-decker structure that resides today was completed in 1971. The Archibald Leitch-designed Main Stand was completed in 1909 — remaining a Goodison fixture until the development of the current structure at the end of the 1960s.

LACE-UP COLLARS

A common trend amongst sides, it was a look that Umbro replicated in the early 1990s on strips including Manchester United's.

FROM GARDEN TO GOAL

FA Cup-winning goalkeeper Billy Scott (centre) was one of the first to utilise what looks like gardening gloves — a trend which failed to catch on in future years.

DID YOU KNOW?

In 1904 the Blues were 5-0 down at half-time to Sheffield Wednesday. They would earn a 5-5 draw, the only instance of a side failing to win when leading by this score at the break. Everton's match at Arsenal in 1904-05 was abandoned due to fog, with the Blues 3-1 up — they lost the eventual 'replay' 2-1, when a win from the original game would have secured the title.

1915 Home

1915 Cutting

EVERTON ROUT THE "GUNNERS."

SKETCHES OF SATURDAY'S CUP-TIE AT GOODISON PARK BY "W.H.D."

1910 Cartoon

THE GREAT TIE AT GOODISON.

SKETCHES ON SATURDAY BY "W.H.D."

1911 Cartoon

EVERTON COLLECTION

Excerpts from the period, from the Everton Collection ledgers:

1906-07
November 13 1906

Jerseys: The Stores Committee were recommended to obtain white wool jerseys with blue neck bands and cuffs as a change jersey.

1908-09
December 1908, Notts County (a) — Boxing Day

Jerseys: Resolved we obtain blue jerseys from J Sharp sample to be submitted and that the directors decide as to what colour the change jersey should be.

18 EFC Kits

1919-1930

Dixie's 60

1919-1930

ABOUT THE KIT

Baggy blue shirt, white shorts and black socks remained as the home strip. The shirt collar would sometimes vary, while a club crest was first spotted on the shirt in the early/mid-20s. By the end of the decade the home shirt had gone modern, with a skin-tight light blue top including a white round collar and two distinct white hoops near the sleeves of each arm. The white shorts had gained a stripe down each side, while the black socks were offset by blue and white-hooped turn-ups. The strip would prove ill-fated, as the Blues were relegated at the end of that campaign.

The away strip was white with blue collar and cuffs, dark blue/black baggies (although white were also used) and black socks with blue hoops.

In terms of the wider picture, the early 20s would see Bukta, seen as a big player as supplier of kits (they had

1920s crest

produced their first football kits, for Nottingham Forest, as far back as 1884) first challenged by Humphrey Brothers Clothing — which became Umbro in 1924. 1921-22 also saw visiting teams required to change colours when kits clashed in Football League games for the first time, while in FA Cup ties both clubs were expected to wear change strips. Numbers on the back of shirts were not yet required to distinguish players, although Arsenal and Chelsea were apparently the first to play in numbered shirts in August 1928.

1929 White away

1929-30 Home

ON-FIELD

League football resumed in 1919 following the First World War. Wilf Chadwick being the league's top scorer in 1923-24 was the highlight of the first part of the 1920s for the Blues, with league form patchy. A fifth-place finish in 22-23 was the high mark, while the season before the Blues had finished 20th — one place above the drop zone. A run to the last eight of the FA Cup in 1921 would also prove the club's best during these 11 seasons.

Of course, the 1927-28 title-winning campaign saw a record 60 First Division goals netted by Dixie Dean. But he actually scored 82 in all competitions that term. Strangely, the season before the success, Everton had again finished 20th. The FA Charity Shield was also won for the first time, a 2-1 victory coming against Blackburn Rovers at Old Trafford. But the period ended in a first relegation, Everton finishing 22nd and bottom one point behind Sheffield United in 20th — a run of four wins in the club's last five not enough.

Mid-1920s Home

OFF-FIELD

The 1919-20 season began with the First and Second Division extended from 20 to 22 clubs. The following campaign saw the Southern League incorporated by the Football League to form the Third Division; 12 months after that leading northern non-league teams were invited to form regional Third Division North and South Leagues. 1926 saw the Bullens Road stand, designed by Archibald Leitch, completed. His criss-cross trademark is still visible today.

Mid-1920s lace neck

EVERTON COLLECTION

Extract taken from club ledgers ahead of 1929-30:

June 11 1929

Jerseys: The question of changing the colour of our jerseys was discussed and it was decided to ask **Mr J Sharp** to obtain samples and submit some to Stores Committee.

1920–1945

1930-1945

Legendary treble

1930-1945

ABOUT THE KIT

The 1929-30 kit featuring the skin-tight shirt was seemingly deemed a failure, as Everton reverted back to the 'baggy' look common at most sides in England. The shirt and shorts 'design' remained a constant, although having reverted back to dark blue, the home shirt may have gone lighter again during the mid and late 1930s (P27). The black home socks varied from a hooped design to white turn-ups.

The 1933 FA Cup final shirts were apparently supplied by Bukta. As well as sporting numbers, both Everton and Manchester City played in change strips — a requisite for cup ties. White was a common change colour for many sides, and Everton were no different. They even played in this strip less than four weeks before, at home to Newcastle, the thinking being that the players could get used to the strip. The

1930s Home

shorts included a white stripe down either side, while the socks were also dark like the shorts, with two lighter-coloured (white?) hoops around the turn-ups. Incidentally, it wasn't until 1939 that numbers on the back of players' shirts became mandatory by the Football League.

1935-36 Home

ON-FIELD

The first three seasons would prove unique in the club's turnaround. A record 121 goals were scored as the Second Division title was collected. That 1930-31 season also saw Dixie Dean score in 12 consecutive games while Everton's biggest league win, 9-1, was equalled - Plymouth Argyle being the unfortunate opposition. The following season, 1931-32, Everton were champions - the first club to win the Second and First Division titles in successive seasons. The latter success yielded successive home wins of 9-3, 8-1, 7-2 and 9-2 - although they lost 12 games, a record high for a title-winning team. In 1932-33, the FA Cup was won, securing a unique treble of Second, First and Cup wins. Dean's successor, Tommy Lawton, was Division One's top scorer in 1937-38 and also in the following campaign, when the title was won. War meant Everton would be champions throughout the period, as they were when the First World War ensured league football ceased at the end of 1914-15.

1933 FA Cup final, change kit

OFF-FIELD

The original two-tier Gwladys Street stand was completed by Archibald Leitch in 1938. It made Goodison Park the first ground in Britain to have four double-decker stands.
Theo Kelly was installed as the club's first official first-team manager in June 1939.

1933 Home

NUMBERS GAME

The 1933 final was the first
official match when numbers
were required. Everton wore
1-11, Manchester City 12-22,
the decision being based on
the toss of a coin.

STRIPED SHORTS

A regular feature of Everton
strips until the mid-1960s,
they were one of the first
clubs to adopt the stripe.

DID YOU KNOW?

Alex Stevenson (1934-1949),
who went on to play for
Rangers, is the only Gers
player to play for the
Republic of Ireland.
Albert Geldard (1932-1938)
was the youngest player to
appear in the League in 1929
(age 15 years, 156 days), a
record that remained intact
until 2008.
The 3-2 loss at Arsenal in
August 1936 was the first
complete match televised.

1931 Team

Circa 1933-36 Home

1935 Home

1938-39 Home

COLLARS, HOOPS

The regular kit incorporated distinctive black socks with hoops on the turn-ups, while a lighter material on the shirt included a button-up collar. A stripe ran down the sides of the white baggy shorts, the almost knee-length a common feature in footballing fashion.

EVERTON COLLECTION

Extracts from club ledgers:

1932-33
December 28 1932

Jerseys and knickers: It was decided to purchase 2 sets of Dark Blue jerseys and white knickers with dark blue facings (?) as our alternative colours.

1934-35
Tuesday September 25 1934

Stockings: It was decided to discontinue the wearing of the perged (?) stockings at present.

November 20 1934

Stocks (?): Samples were submitted and it was decided to order...pairs of the navy blue stockings with white tops.

1945-1950
Post-war recovery

1945-1950

ABOUT THE KIT

Clothing rationing after the Second World War meant little change to strips in general, with clubs limited in replacing their kits. Indeed, some sides were forced to change from traditional colours to those purchased with ration coupons. For example, West Brom apparently wore plain blue; Oldham sported red and white hooped jerseys borrowed from the local rugby league club; and Southport played in green and white hoops for several seasons, a gift from one of the club's directors. Everton's home strip remained a constant, with baggy shirt and generous open-necked collar with the white pre-Second World War shorts. Socks were again the one variable, blue with white turn-ups or white hoops. The away strip remained white with black shorts and socks, with white turn-ups.

1947 Home

1950 Home

ON-FIELD

The period was a barren one for the club, with a sole run to the semi-finals of the FA Cup in 1950 being the one real cause of excitement — the Blues going down 2-0 to Liverpool at Maine Road. In the league, Everton did not finish higher than 10th, with Ephraim 'Jock' Dodds top scorer between 1946-48, and Eddie Wainwright likewise between 1948-50.

Sanctioned league football did not begin again until 46-47 (the season they recorded their highest league finish), although the FA Cup did resume the season before. The FA decided to make ties from round one to round six two-legged affairs — an experiment that lasted only one season. The idea was to give all teams a chance, due to some sides being depleted due to players still being involved in the war effort. The Blues went out to Preston 4-3 on aggregate in round one, the home second leg extending beyond the 10 minutes each way of extra-time. Seven minutes into sudden death a certain Bill Shankly would hit

1950 action v West Brom

the winning penalty. It was the last opposition penalty scored at Goodison Park in the competition, until James Milner's spot-kick for Aston Villa in 2009.

These years did see one notable record set - which still exists today. Peter Farrell's goal at Liverpool on Christmas Eve 1949 is unofficially timed at 12 seconds — the quickest goal in the Blues' history.

OFF-FIELD

Welsh inside-forward Aubrey Powell became one of Everton's first record signings of the post-Second World War period, joining from Leeds United in the summer of 1948. He would go on to score only five goals in 35 games for the club.

Cliff Britton replaced Theo Kelly as manager in September 1948.

FAMOUS MATCH
Everton 1-1 Liverpool
(Division One).

NUMBERS GAME

The requirement for numbers on shirts was standardised by the FA ahead of the 1939–40 season — which lasted only three games due to war. This shot, from 1950, shows Everton's No 2 defending against West Ham's No 9.

CLUB CREST

This 1949 shot of Ted Common shows the old crest displayed on the strip, like on shirts in the 1920s - although the Blues' first-team jersey did not display any logos until the 1970s.

DID YOU KNOW?

The above game in 1948 remains the biggest official attendance at Goodison Park — and on Merseyside — of 78,299 official spectators. Peter Corr (1948–49), who was uncle of the four members of Irish band The Corrs, was also part of the Ireland team to defeat England 2-0 at Goodison in 1949 - the first non-UK team to beat the national side on English soil.

1949-50

NEW MATERIAL?

Woollen round-necked jumpers were still the norm for keepers, with gloves rarely worn. Any that were used would be to keep hands warm rather than offering any real advantages to the wearer. Often the full kit was at the discretion of the player, with these shots (below centre and far left) showing different coloured shorts, and a cap being worn in 1950 by George Burnett. Cotton material and button collars were common for outfielders, as shown in the 1949-50 team pic. Jock Dodds (below) appears to be in training top, as signified by the mystery No 30 scribbled on the shirt.

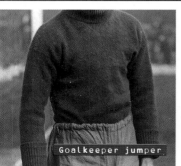

Goalkeeper jumper

1950 Keeper

Training top

1950-1955
Ups and downs

1950-1955

50-55 PLAYERS Dave Hickson, T.E. Jones, Tommy Eglington
MANAGER Cliff Britton

ABOUT THE KIT

The general trend for collared shirts became standard. Hooped socks became popular, while Everton maintained their traditional home colours, with only minor alterations to the shirt collar. Blue socks with white-turn-ups became a regular feature. The white away strip again remained relatively unchanged, while a new strip was sported in 1952-53 — a trip to face Huddersfield, in their usual blue and white stripes, saw Everton turn out in what appears to be a yellow shirt with black collar, black shorts and black and yellow hooped socks. Did it prove lucky? The 'Yellows' lost 8-2.

The 1953 FA Cup final saw Bolton sport a kit made from a shiny material, apparently the first time artificial fabric had been used in the manufacture of shirts and shorts. Torquay United are said to be one of the first to adopt the style the following season.

The first pale socks first appeared at some clubs, and by the end of the decade, white socks became more widely used.

1951 Home

1955 Home

ON-FIELD

It was one of the darkest periods for the club in terms of league football, with the Blues being relegated for only the second (and last) time in their history. They came 22nd in 1950-51, bottom of the table despite finishing level on points with the two teams directly above them. The final day saw the Blues capitulate 6-0 at Sheffield Wednesday who, despite the result, also went down with Everton.

The club spent three subsequent seasons in the second tier, the 16th-place finish in 1952-53 being their lowest-ever placing.

Ironically, that season also saw a memorable run to the semi-finals of the FA Cup – their best in the competition during the period. The run saw memorable wins over Manchester United and Aston Villa before Bolton Wanderers prevailed 4-3 in the last-four clash at Maine Road — the Trotters had been four-up at the interval.

The following season saw promotion achieved, Everton finishing as runners-up only on goal difference to

1950-51 Line-up

Early 1950s Home & keeper

champions Leicester City. Mid-table consolidation followed in 1954-55, their first season back in the top flight, and first of 55 consecutive campaigns at the top level, ahead of 2009-10. John Willie Parker finished as the club's top scorer for four consecutive seasons from 1951-52.

OFF-FIELD

Harry Potts became the club's record signing in the autumn of 1950 for £20,000. It was a figure that would stand for nearly eight years.

The great Ted Sagar made his final first-team appearance for the club in November 1952 against Plymouth Argyle, age 42 years and nine months.

BLUE SOCKS

Blue with white turn-ups was the norm for home strips, rather than previous incarnations - namely black socks, or blue with white hoops.

EXCITING NO 10 SHIRT

John Willie Parker, Everton's most prolific goalscorer during the period, in action during the 1953 FA Cup quarter-final at Aston Villa.

DID YOU KNOW?

Four Everton players represented the Republic of Ireland for the first time in the same match in November 1953. Tommys Clinton and Eglington, Peter Farrell and goalkeeper Jimmy O'Neill started in a 1-0 defeat to France in a World Cup qualifier. This happened another three times during the period, Dan Donovan replacing Tommy Clinton in the foursome.

1950-1955

1953 Keeper

1953 Yellow?

CHANGES

White shirt, with black shorts and black socks with white turn-ups continued to be used as a change strip. However, the strip worn at Huddersfield (left) in April 1953 is one of the first pictorial examples of the club wearing a change strip other than white. Of course, Everton travelled to other clubs as well as the Terriers, such as QPR and Blackburn before this season, so it is plausible to suggest that yellow/amber or another alternative could have been sported before this campaign. The picture far left shows another developing trend — keeper in black, rather than the home white shorts.

1950-51 Away

1954-55 Away

1955-1962

Mersey Millionaires

1955 - 1962

1955-1962

55-62 PLAYERS Bobby Collins, Jimmy Harris, Roy Vernon
MANAGERS Cliff Britton, Ian Buchan, Johnny Carey, Harry Catterick

ABOUT THE KIT

Continental influences began to creep into the English game in the form of new lightweight strips featuring V-necks, short sleeves and more streamlined shorts. This was reflected in Everton's new kit designs, although they began to wear a round-neck design from 1961 onwards. The modernisation of the away strips appeared less of a priority, with the V-neck not introduced until at least a season after the home design. Change kits continued to be worn in the FA Cup, for teams whose home colours clashed. For example, 1961/62 saw Everton play non-League King's Lynn at Goodison in a change kit. On this occasion it was a yellow/amber top with black round-neck, black shorts and yellow/amber socks, which included black hooped turn-ups. Club ledgers also indicate a fluorescent shirt being worn (P43) four seasons before.

1956 Home

1962 Home

ON-FIELD

The rest of the 50s signified on-field mediocrity, with the Blues finishing 15th or 16th in five successive seasons. It was a period which saw Wally Fielding become the oldest player to score for the club in a first-team game, v West Brom age 38 years, 305 days. It was only an injection of cash from Littlewoods impressario John Moores that ignited the club, providing vital on-field investment that allowed Everton to flourish. They finished fifth in 1960-61, their best post-war finish to date - but it was not enough for Moores, who asked Johnny Carey to step down, famously in the back of a taxi on the way to a meeting with the FA.

Harry Catterick was brought in, having enjoyed success with Sheffield Wednesday. His first season saw Everton finish fourth, winning 17 of 21 home games and only five points behind surprise champions Ipswich. Roy Vernon finished with 28 goals from 40 games. A year before, the club also reached the FA Youth Cup for the first time.

1957 v Man City away

1959 Away

OFF-FIELD

A period of manager upheaval saw Ian Buchan replace Cliff Britton in 1956; Johnny Carey came in in 1958; and Harry Catterick, in April 1961. Floodlights were installed at Goodison Park in 1957, with undersoil heating a further addition a year later. Bobby Collins joined for a new club-record fee in 1958.

EVERTON COLLECTION

Extract from 1957-58 season:

October 1 1957

Jerseys: It was reported that the fluorescent jerseys had been satisfactory at Bolton, and that a set had been ordered. (N.B. There was no game at Bolton — was it the reserves or youth team?)

THE MODERN LOOK

A 1961 Goodison friendly v Dynamo Kiev was amongst the matches Everton's all white away kit was worn. The shirt included a modern gold and blue 'strip' across the chest.

THIRD KIT?

Games at Ipswich and Burnley, as pictured here, saw Everton wear a yellow and black strip, rather than the usual blue or white, in the early 60s.

DID YOU KNOW?

October 1958 saw the club go down 10-4 at Tottenham, the most goals conceded by the Blues in a first-team game. Later that year, Goodison Park was the first stadium with undersoil heating to beat the winter frost. Everton did not win an away game in the 1959-60 season. Jimmy Harris was the club's first League Cup goalscorer, against Accrington Stanley, in 1960-61.

1962 Keeper

1956-57 Squad

COLLAR TO V TO U-NECK

The main trend was for lighter shirts, V-neck and 'U-neck' collars. Research has brought to light team photos where both collared shirts and V-neck are worn in the 55-56 campaign, although there is no disputing a definitive shift to the more modern approach the following season (left). The same applied for the away shirts, although a black collar, as well as V and U-neck were worn at differing times during the period. Round neck seemed to become the norm by 1961-62. Goalkeeper tops became thinner again in material, as highlighted in the shot (far left) of Albert Dunlop in 1962.

1959 Third

1956-57 Away

1957-58 Away

1962-1966
League and cup glory

1962-1966

ABOUT THE KIT

In 1960s Britain the trend was for shirts to become tighter, shorts 'shorter' and socks more lightweight. Simplified design was the norm, while plain kits stood out better under floodlights — which were now universal. Coventry City were apparently the first side to adopt matching shirts and shorts in 1962 (excluding the white change kits used or the colours used by Swansea, for example).

The main change in Everton's home strip, as well as from short to long sleeves, was from predominantly white socks to blue for the home kit, which had been adopted by the time of the FA Charity Shield in 1963. These socks were also worn with an all white away kit at West Ham in October, and in the British Championship first-leg at Rangers in November — both in 1963. Incidentally, the all white, with blue and gold strip

1962–63 Home

across the chest of the shirt, was last worn at West Ham in April 1963. Another example of change strips at Goodison was in the the 1966 FA Cup quarter-final, Everton v Manchester City. Both clubs wore their away kits - the Blues sported white round-neck tops, black shorts and white socks.

1963–64 Home

1963–64 Away (home socks)

ON-FIELD

As well as clinching the 1962–63 championship — the club's first post-war success — it is the only campaign the Blues have gone through the entire league season unbeaten at home. The average crowd that term of 51,603 also remains the club's best, although their first season in European compeition ended at the first hurdle, Jock Stein's Dunfermline Athletic causing a shock by going through 2–1 on aggregate in the Inter-Cities Fairs Cup. The Blues secured the FA Charity Shield in the curtain raiser to the following season by sweeping aside Manchester United 4–0, although their first European Cup adventure ended at the first stage. In the days before seedings, Italian champions Inter Milan went through 1–0 on aggregate (the second leg in the San Siro seeing 18-year-old Colin Harvey make his debut). The Italians would go on the win the trophy for two consecutive years.
There were two other Fairs Cup campaigns (the Blues reaching rounds three and

1963–64 European Cup

two), while in Division One there were finishes of third and fourth. They were 11th in 65–66, but made up for this by winning the FA Cup for the third time. The 3–2 win over Sheffield Wednesday remains one of the most memorable in the competition's history, the Blues having come back from a two-goal deficit. Other notable moments saw a 12–1 win for the youth side over their Wigan Athletic counterparts in 1964 — the club's record FA Youth Cup win, and a first success in that competition in 1964–65.

OFF-FIELD

Tony Kay became Britain's most expensive player when he signed from Sheffield Wednesday in 1962. Two years later, he became embroiled in a betting scandal along with two other ex-Owls team-mates. He was fined and served 10 weeks in prison. Upon release, he was banned from football for seven years.
The club's first European Cup match saw stand prices rise — the club's explanation? 'If supporters wish to see world-class teams they need to pay the going rate.'

FAMOUS MATCH
Everton 3-2 Sheffield Wednesday
(FA Cup final).

FA CUP SEMI-FINAL

Brian Labone leads the team out ahead of the 1966 tie v Manchester United — although the game, like the final at Wembley, wasn't given any special kit recognition.

THE MAGIC NUMBER

Original printed No 3 from the mid-1960s home shirt.

DID YOU KNOW?

Dennis Stevens was Everton's first European goalscorer, netting the winner in a 1-0 Inter-Cities Fairs Cup first -leg win over Dunfermline. John Hurst became the club's first substitute in a league match, replacing Fred Pickering in a 1-1 draw at Stoke City in August 1965. Everton defender Ray Wilson was the oldest member of England's victorious 1966 World Cup side.

1966 FA Cup S-F

1963 Amber

EVERTON COLOURS

The trend for yellow/amber change shirts began to become more apparent, with the colour convenient at West Bromwich Albion in May 1963 (left) — with white, rather than black shorts. The usual white and black was unusually worn at Goodison, in the 1966 FA Cup quarter-final against Manchester City (below, left). Goalkeeper Gordon West sports green jersey (no gloves), black shorts and the usual blue socks with white turn-ups (below middle left and centre), while Everton's 1966 cup semi-final mascot proudly sports a homemade No 9 (far left).

1966 Away

1964 Keeper

1966 FA Cup final

1966-1972
Highs and lows

1966-1972

66-72 PLAYERS Joe Royle, Alan Ball, Howard Kendall
MANAGER Harry Catterick

ABOUT THE KIT

There was little change in the club's home strip, with cotton long-sleeved blue shirts with white round neck and white shorts as standard. Socks also reverted back to plain white by 1967-68. Amber socks were the other home strip addition if colours clashed with the opposition in away games, examples of which include the 1968 FA Cup semi and games at Arsenal and Spurs. Everton actually played a part in this rule being brought in following a mid-1960s visit to Chelsea. Having brought no alternative to their usual white socks, they were forced to wear the home side's yellow away stockings. Amber shirts, blue shorts and amber socks became the main away strip, as can be seen right (1967-68 Home & Away) — the action being from a then traditional firsts v seconds pre-season game. The strip —

1970 Original

1967-68 Home & Away

1966-67 Home

1969-70 Home

but with blue socks — was worn at Goodison for an FA Cup tie against Colchester in 1971, as well as at Wembley in the 1968 Cup final. During 71-72 though, green shorts with amber shirt and socks was worn at Chelsea and Leicester. White reverted to a third strip, with blue socks worn when socks clashed.

1966-1972

ON-FIELD

The 1969-70 title success proved the highlight, the Blues claiming a record club points total of 66 (two points for a win). The 29 wins from 42 is also the best achieved by Everton in a season. Chronologically, from 1966-67, Harry Catterick's side finished 6th, 5th, 3rd, 1st, 14th and 15th.

The FA Cup final provided disappointment in 1968, with the favourites going down 1-0 after extra-time against West Brom. The Blues also reached the last four in 1969 and 1971 — in the latter year, for one season only, a third/ fourth place play-off was played. Everton were beaten in this, 3-2 by Stoke City.

Defeated by Liverpool in the 1966 FA Charity Shield, four years later champions Everton won 2-1 at Chelsea.

There was again little to shout about in Europe, with the 1970-71 European Cup run ending in the quarter-finals, while 1966-67 saw Cup Winners' Cup defeat in round two. Other notable moments include the 8-0 defeat of Southampton in 1971, which remains a post-

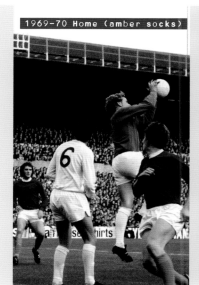

1969-70 Home (amber socks)

war Everton best. Joe Royle and Alan Ball were the prolific marksmen, the former scoring 29 in 1968-69 before notching another 23 in 69-70. In the four seasons from 1966-67, Ball hit 18, 20, 18 and 12. Brian Labone made the last of his 534 appearances — the record for an Everton outfield player — against Chelsea in August 1971.

1971 FA Cup quarter-final

OFF-FIELD

The 1968 FA Cup final would be the first to be televised live in colour.

The Main Stand at Goodison was completed in 1971, becoming the first three-tier structure in England.

Alan Ball was allowed to leave for a British record fee of £220,000 in December 1971.

1966-1972

SUCCESS IN AMBER

Although beaten wearing their change strip in the 1968 FA Cup final, Everton did pick up some silverware in the kit two years later, in the form of the FA Charity Shield.

WHITE V BLUE...SOCKS

The great Alan Ball pictured in an Everton 'third' strip, against Burnley, in 1967.

DID YOU KNOW?

The first FA Cup tie shown on closed-circuit TV was at Anfield, the FA Cup fifth-round home tie against Liverpool being beamed back in March 1967. The combined Goodison and Anfield attendances amounted to 105,000 – the biggest single attendance for an FA Cup tie, other than the final.
In 2007, The Times rated the home strip No 45 in their top 50 best kits of all time.

1967 Keeper

1969 Cup SF

ALL THE RANGE

The amber `jinx` was
maintained in 1969 (left)
when a late goal saw the Blues
beaten in the FA Cup
semi-final by Manchester City.
The Holy Trinity are pictured
in the traditional royal blue
(below), with Alan Ball the
first to leave in December
1971, while there was a first
sighting of goalkeeper Gordon
West in gloves, in what looks
suspiciously like gardening
`mittens`, at Stamford Bridge
in a league game.

1966-72 Home

1966-1972

1972-1974

Changing times

1972-1974

72 PLAYERS John Connolly, John Hurst, Terry Darracott
MANAGERS Harry Catterick, Tommy Eggleston (caretaker), Billy Bingham

ABOUT THE KIT

The period saw the first
'writing' on the Everton shirt,
namely the legend 'EFC' in
italics in a small diagonal
design. The long-standing white
round neck, a predominantly
1960s addition, was replaced by
a 'flappy' white collar and
white 'V' inset. It was a design
apparently first used at the
end of the 1960s by Aston Villa
(although this had first
appeared during the 1950s, and
was worn by Hearts the
following decade).
As well as an amber and blue
away kit in the same design
including EFC legend, a third
strip was again worn on
occasion, being white with blue
flappy collar and filled-in
corresponding V-neck, white
shorts and white socks with
blue hoop on the turn-up of the
white socks.

1972-74 Home

1972-74 Away

1972-1974

60 EFC Kits

ON-FIELD

After beginning the season unbeaten in their first eight league games, the 1972-73 season quickly unravelled. Out of the League Cup at the first hurdle, a shock FA Cup fourth-round exit at the hands of Millwall at Goodison meant Everton's search for silverware had ended in the first week of February. Harry Catterick's health had also deteriorated, and his assistant Tommy Egglestone stepped in for the final few games of the campaign. The Blues finished 17th, with no player reaching double figures in terms of goals. The Cat was subsequently moved upstairs, made a non-executive director of the club, signalling the end of his 12-year managerial tenure. After a prolonged search for a replacement, Billy Bingham was installed as new manager.

The former midfield favourite took Everton to seventh in his first season in charge, and although goals proved again in short supply, Bob Latchford was brought in in mid-season from Birmingham City, netting

1972 Friendly, v Falkirk

seven in 13 games. Unfortunately, the cups again proved fruitless in terms of tangible reward, with early exits coming in the FA Cup, League Cup and Texaco Cup, the latter being an early-70s competition for UK clubs who had failed to qualify for one of the three European club tournaments.

OFF-FIELD

Bob Latchford signed from Birmingham for a British transfer record of £350,000 in 1974. As part of the deal, Howard Kendall and Archie Styles moved to St Andrew's. Harry Catterick would cut his ties with the club in 1975. He would take over the managerial reigns at Preston.

1972-1974

FAMOUS MATCH
Everton 0-0 West Bromwich Albion
(FA Cup fourth round).

FIRST LOGO?

The Latin-style `E.F.C.` was a departure for the Everton kits, the first logo ever sported by the first team. Or was this shirt (below right) ever worn competitively in the 1920s?

COLLAR OF THE TIMES

The white V-design collar on the royal blue home shirt would be a touch replicated in the mid-1980s on the Le Coq Sportif home shirt.

DID YOU KNOW?

Everton's 3-2 win at Norwich in November 1973 is the only game involving the Blues to feature own goals from both sides — John McLaughlin for the Canaries, and Duncan Forbes for Everton.
The FA Cup fourth-round tie with West Brom on January 27, 1974 created history. The goalless draw against the Baggies was the first time the Blues had played a competitive Sunday fixture.

1972-73 Reserves

70S FASHIONS

Gloves again appeared an optional choice for keepers, as highlighted below. The top generally worn by Everton stoppers was green, with the cloth material featureless — be it no logos or elbow padding. The plain white shorts and socks were those worn by the first team, a relative departure particularly from previous Everton goalkeepers, who would often sport black shorts. Often too the top would not feature a number. This page also features reserve action (left), with the Everton side yet to adopt the modern home strip.

1972-74 Away number

1972 Cov collar v EFC collar

1972-1974

1974-1976
Carlisle, home and away

1974-1976

74-76 PLAYERS Roger Kenyon, Mike Bernard, Mick Buckley
MANAGER Billy Bingham

ABOUT THE KIT

Umbro officially become the club's kit manufacturer — in terms of `on-shirt` recognition. The only obvious change to the kit was the unmistakeable Umbro diamond opposite the `EFC` legend, initially made up of white, black and blue stitching — but later just white. Shorts were white with blue Umbro diamond, with home socks white — and change socks blue.

The away strip, of amber with blue flappy collar and filled-in `v`, again incorporated a latin-style `EFC` diagonal, with an Umbro diamond logo. Blue shorts, and blue socks were also worn, for example at Leicester City in March 1976. It was in these early days of kit manufacturers, with kit sponsors looking to best display their logos, that led to the classic Umbro sleeves.

1974-75 Home

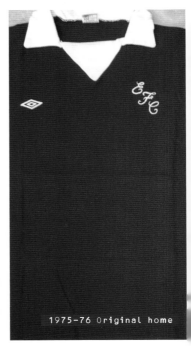

1975-76 Original home

1974-1976

ON-FIELD

It would be a case of so near, yet so far in 1974-75. The Blues would finish fourth in Division One, only three points behind champions Derby County. A run of only two wins in their last 10 games did not help matters in the final reckoning. However newly-promoted Carlisle United, who ended up finishing rock-bottom, did an unlikely double against Everton, winning 3-2 at Goodison Park after being two-down, while they eased to a 3-0 win at Brunton Park. In cold, hard statistical terms, had those four points (it was still two for a win up until the 1981-82 season) lost been won, the club would have won the championship. The Blues also lost fewer league games than anyone else that season. A shock home defeat came at the hands of Fulham in the last 16 of the FA Cup, and eventual winners Aston Villa were victors after a replay in the second round of the League Cup. Bob Latchford would also finish as top scorer with 19, with Mick Lyons netting 11 goals. The following season saw an

1974-75 Home

unspectacular 11th-place finish — an eight-match winless run in November and early December banishing any potential title challenge. Cup disappointments came against Derby County (FA Cup), Notts County (League Cup) and AC Milan (UEFA Cup), while top scorer Latchford was the only player to reach double figures.

1975-76 Original number

1975-76 Original collar

OFF-FIELD

Colin Harvey made the last of his 300+ Everton appearances in a 1-1 draw at Stoke in August 1974 — he moved on to Sheffield Wednesday.
The January FA Cup fourth-round trip to Plymouth Argyle in January 1975 (above, left) saw Everton backed by over 7,000 fans.

FAMOUS MATCH
Everton 3-2 Leeds United
(Division One).

STYLO

Everton trainer Stewart Imlach supplemented his earnings with a sponsorship deal with 'football shoe' company Stylo Matchmakers.

KIT LOGOS

The first official Umbro shirt, made distinctive from the generic 'blue'. The 'EFC' legend, now without full stops, would remain a staple until 1978.

DID YOU KNOW?

It was Leeds United in 1975 who produced the first replica kit that could be sold to fans, after entering into a deal with Admiral. The same year Manchester United also adopted Admiral as kit sponsors, and a public outcry followed the news fans would have to shell out £15 for an authentic United top instead of the £5 that would have yielded a generic red shirt with white trim.

1975-76 Away

FULL SET

Simple yet distinctly Everton, whether royal blue or amber. Even in the club's first season of logo recognition, 1974-75 (below), the kit seemed somehow ahead of its time — well, compared to non-League Altrincham, who'd just earned an unlikely replay at Goodison in the FA Cup. The amber/yellow shirt with blue trim would usually be worn with blue shorts and amber/yellow or blue socks, depending upon clashes with the home side.

The goalkeeper? A resolutely plain green, again with gloves deemed as optional.

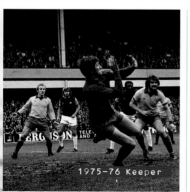
1975-76 Keeper

1974-75 Home

1976-1977

Lee, Lyons, Latchford, luck

1976-1977

76-77 PLAYERS Mick Lyons, Ken McNaught, Duncan McKenzie
MANAGERS Billy Bingham, Gordon Lee

ABOUT THE KIT

The first classic Umbro sleeves shirt, with the updated Umbro shirt logo one of the other noticeable changes. The previous V-collar was opened up, while opposite the Umbro was the legend `E.F.C.´ (the full stops returning) — in simple horizontal text. A blue Umbro diamond pattern ran down the sides of the white shorts, while the strip was completed by plain white socks. Clubs with similar designed kits included then fellow top-flight side Bristol City. There were also blue shorts with white Umbro diamonds worn when the Blues were away from home against sides who played in white shorts. Occasions such as the League Cup semi-final second leg at Bolton saw the Blues' home kit revert to blue socks — again, due to a clash with the home side's socks.

The away strip was an all amber affair with blue Umbro diamonds across the sleeves, a V-neck shirt with `flappy´ collar and blue sleeve ends. The diamond pattern was also repeated on the shorts, with plain amber socks.

1977 FA Cup S-F

1976-77 Blue shorts

1976-1977

ON-FIELD

Gordon Lee's arrival in early 1977, due mainly to inconsistent league form under Billy Bingham, came at an unusual time, with Everton still involved in both domestic cup competitions. Indeed, a 1-0 win at Bolton Wanderers in the League Cup semi-final, second leg would earn a first final in the competition, against Aston Villa. It went to a third game, with the Blues unfortunate to go down 3-2 after extra-time at Old Trafford.

Everton also enjoyed a run to the FA Cup semi-finals for the first time in six years, although again, Liverpool would end the club's Wembley dream in a replay — this after a late Bryan Hamilton 'winning' goal was chalked off for 'handball' by FIFA-approved ref Clive Thomas. In Division One, a ninth-place finish was secured, while Bob Latchford (25) and Andy King (12) were the top marksmen. The youth team would also reach the FA Youth Cup final for a second time, going down to Crystal Palace in a tight two-legged affair.

Team shot, early-1977

OFF-FIELD

Boss Billy Bingham was replaced by caretaker-manager Steve Burtenshaw in January, with the Blues lying 13th in Division One. He was winless in his four games in charge, before Gordon Lee left Newcastle United to take over the Goodison hot seat at the end of that month.

1977 League Cup final

FINAL LOGO

An original shirt, as worn in the 1977 League Cup final. For the first time, the royal blue sported not only a cup final logo — but 'Umbro' wording.

WHAT'S OUR NAME?

The tracksuit legend — in case anyone was in any doubt.

DID YOU KNOW?

Duncan McKenzie and Bruce Rioch were signed in December 1976 by Billy Bingham. A month later, he was replaced as boss by Gordon Lee. Both players had left the club within two years of signing.

The first match of the 1977 League Cup final was deemed so poor in quality that ITV chose not to screen the planned highlights of the match the following day.

1976-1977

FIRSTS V RESERVES

1976-77 1sts v 2nds

The August 1976 game between the first team and second string was one of the last ever played at Goodison. An early season game between the Blues and Aston Villa at Goodison (below) — who would meet three times to decide the outcome of the League Cup final — shows an early example of Umbro using a similar design template in their kits. As well as shirt logos, the unmistakeable diamonds were sported on both clubs' shorts — Everton's in blue, Villa's in their usual claret home colour. Strangely Villa were permitted to also wear their white home shorts.

1976-77 Away

1976-77 Home

1977-1979

Hitting 30

1977-1979

77-79 PLAYERS Bob Latchford, Andy King, Martin Dobson
MANAGER Gordon Lee

ABOUT THE KIT

There was little change in the home strip in 1977-78, except in the Umbro sleeves, with the Umbro logo now closely matching the symbol of the kit manufacturer. In terms of the change strip, all amber was generally used as sported at West Ham, for example. The Umbro touches replicated the home strip — although the logo remained without the Umbro text on the shirt and shorts. It was the same kit as worn the previous season.

The 1978-79 season would be the last before shirt sponsorship was permitted by the FA. The official club crest was also incorporated on the shirt for the first time, within a white beer mat-style circle patch. It is thus the first season when the club's motto, "Nil Satis Nisi Optimum" (translated roughly as: `Nothing but the

1978-79 Home

best is good enough") was first displayed on the shirt. However, match programmes from the season suggest Hafnia (owned by JAKA Foods Group Ltd, New Brighton) was already involved with the club, sponsoring the 'Star Portraits' pull-out series.

Away from home, blue socks were worn with the home shirt and shorts (above, right) when there was a clash with the home team — in this instance, at Manchester United.

1978-79 Blue shorts

1977-1979

ON-FIELD

Bob Latchford's 30 league goals in 1977-78 was the first time the total had been reached by any First Division player in seven years. The 'Goodison Opinion' piece from the Newcastle United programme (October 29 1977) had told of how Bob was rated at odds of 100-1 to become the first player to score 30 league goals in either the First or Second Divisions — and scoop the Daily Express's £10,000 prize. Bob commented: "I got 26 last season. And given reasonable freedom from injuries, I would hope to reach 30 this time in all games." He would actually score 32 in all competitions while Andy King and Duncan McKenzie scored 11, as Everton finished third in Division One, while in the domestic cup competitions Everton's best efforts were a run to the quarter-finals.
As well as an 8-0 demolition of Wimbledon in the League Cup in August 1978-79 — the last time the Blues have hit eight in competitive action — the Blues remained unbeaten in the league from April to December 1978, a run of 20 matches. They would

1977-78 Away

eventually finish fourth, running out of steam in winning only two of their last 13 league games. In the UEFA Cup, Czech side Dukla Prague proved too strong at the second-round stage, while there were also early exits in the FA Cup (Sunderland) and League Cup (to Nottingham Forest).

OFF-FIELD

A new Safety Act meant the first home game of 1977-78 against Nottingham Forest saw capacity restricted to below 40,000. The season also began with the boys' pen removed, a measure taken in order to help restore capacity to 56,000 by complying with the Safety of Sports Grounds Act.

FAMOUS MATCH
Everton 6-0 Chelsea
(Division One).

LONG SLEEVES
Dave Thomas shows off the
Umbro diamonds as he lies on
the Bolton turf in agony
during a 3-1 defeat at
Burnden Park in April 1979.

EUROPEAN TOUR
No special commemorative
strips for the 1978-79 UEFA
Cup campaign, just the home
kit for their tie against a
Dukla Prague (third) kit.

DID YOU KNOW?

The Everton v Manchester City
game, on October 1 1977, saw
the match sponsored by
Merseyside company 'Brook
Hire' — the first time this
had happened. The economic
climate of football was cited
as a major factor in this
development, as reflected in
the 'Goodison Opinion' column
in the match programme:
'The financial problems of
League football are well aired
in the Press and on television
and clubs are always on the
lookout for additional sources
of revenue. Sponsorship is a
new form of revenue as far as
we are concerned, but we also
intend to make it something
more than an additional source
of income.'
The year 1977 also saw
Scottish side Hibernian become
the first top-level British
club to wear shirts carrying
sponsorship (Bukta, their kit
manufacturer). Derby County
would land the first English
agreement with Saab, although
the sponsored shirts were
never worn after the
pre-season photo shoot ahead
of 1977-78.

1978-79 Keeper

1978-79 Anfield derby

BOY GEORGE

Scotland goalkeeper George Wood was an ever-present for Everton during this period. A bright green long-sleeved cotton shirt was the normal top — a common colour throughout the English League. The shirt logos would replicate the usual kit, although the collar harked back to earlier in the decade, with the flappy collar and V-neck collar pattern. In the picture (far left) he is wearing the change shorts, worn by the team at Southampton. One noticeable 'advancement' is the use of modern goalkeeping gloves.

1978-79 Latch perm

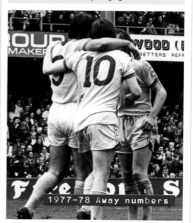

1977-78 Away numbers

1977–1979

1979-1982
All change

1979-1982

79-82 PLAYERS John Bailey, Billy Wright, Asa Hartford
MANAGERS Gordon Lee, Howard Kendall

ABOUT THE KIT

The Hafnia logo became a shirt fixture for non-televised games — the sponsorship deal yielding massive exposure over the next six years. The Football League initially limited the logo size to a two-and-a-half inch strip, to placate fans and the BBC, with their 'non-advertising' policy. For all televised games, FA Cup ties and European fixtures, broadcasters refused to televise clubs who sported sponsors' logo — thus shirts were unbranded for TV coverage. During the period, upon being forced to revert to a sponsor-less shirt at Derby (a 1-0 win) due to the presence of BBC TV cameras, Mick Lyons was said to have claimed: "It was a pity. I quite like the new shirts — in fact, they look better to me." The kit remained the same until 1981-82, when the blue socks reverted to white (although

this trend was reversed on occasion before then — as shown for the home game against Ipswich Town (below right). The away strip, all yellow with blue trim, did not change though an all-white alternative was introduced by 1981. It incorporated a V-neck, blue and white cricket collar-style design, blue trim on shorts and plain white socks. Blue shorts with white trim were also worn, when colour clashes permitted. Umbro's logo was also included on the shorts — without text.

1980-81 Home (FA Cup)

1979-80 Home (non-TV)

1979-80 White socks

ON-FIELD

The first season of 'Hafnia' would see Everton finish 19th, one place and four points above the relegation zone. Only two away games were won, and after finishing 15th in 80-81 — but only three points off the bottom three — Gordon Lee left. His successor would be former midfield legend Howard Kendall, who in the first season of three points for a win, guided the Blues to eighth place.

The cup competitions yielded a semi-final and quarter-final appearance. In the 1980 FA Cup, a last-gasp Frank Lampard Snr winner dashed Everton's hopes, 2-1 after extra-time against West Ham in an Elland Road replay. The following season, Manchester City went through in a Maine Road last-eight replay. There was another season in Europe in 1979-80, but again the club did not distinguish themselves in continental competition, Feyenoord winning 2-0 on aggregate in the UEFA Cup first round. From 1979-80, Brian Kidd (17), Peter Eastoe (19) and Graeme Sharp (15) were top scorers.

Hitachi v Hafnia, 1979

OFF-FIELD

The Opinion feature noted in the first programme of 1979/80: 'Our shirts are sponsored by the Hafnia Ham Company, a Merseyside-based firm which has been closely associated with Everton for some time. Their parent company, Jaka Foods, sponsored two games in each of the last two seasons. Hafnia's managing director, Mr Ollie Toft, is also a very keen supporter of the club.'

The great Dixie Dean passed away at the Goodison derby match of March 1980.

Howard Kendall replaced Gordon Lee, initially as player-boss in May 1981, having impressed at Blackburn Rovers.

FAMOUS MATCH
Everton 2-1 Liverpool
(FA Cup fourth round).

PLAIN WHITE

Shirt numbering would remain a simple preserve, free of kit manufacturer's logos and (apart from European games) 1-11 plus sub(s) — until Le Coq Sportif took over in 1983.

POPULAR TEDDY

Spotted during Everton's open-top bus tour of the city in 1985, the Hafnia-less kit remained a favourite.

DID YOU KNOW?

In February 1981, goalkeeper Jim McDonagh mistakenly wore his Hafnia-emblazoned jersey for the second half of the game with Crystal Palace — highlights of which were to be screened on the BBC's *Match of the Day*. When it was shown that evening, so the legend goes, viewers saw the keeper from a side angle only. The ban on shirt advertising on TV would be lifted by the middle of the decade.

1980 FA Cup S-F Replay

1979-80 Away

SHIRT SPONSORSHIP

The issue was noted in the first home programme of 1979/80, v Norwich City — the first time Hafnia was sported.

'As with most innovations, we realise that some might not give full approval to this advertising. It is not possible to run a major club nowadays unless every commercial avenue is investigated.

'Anticipating the financial potential of advertising on shirts, we joined Bolton Wanderers two years ago in pioneering a change in the Football Association rules governing this subject.

'We are confident the long-term benefits will be considerable and, one day, shirt advertising will be accepted as part of the normal football scene.'

Secretary Jim Greenwood also commented: "Since our success in changing the rules, we have been holding back on a decision to link up with a sponsor for our shirts. This was because the TV companies made it known that they would not be prepared to accept such advertising.

"We have been pressing the Football League for some 12 months to seek TV approval for the shirt advertising. Up to date, we have not achieved success but our efforts will continue.

"In the mean time, we have decided that a start must be made, and if others follow, as we confidently expect, then our campaign will be that much stronger. We predict that most clubs will be involved by the end of the season and, in that event, we would have a strong argument to put before the League and TV companies."

FIRSTS?

Although Liverpool were the first professional club to agree to a 'permitted' shirt sponsorship, with Japanese firm Hitachi in the summer of 1979, non-league Kettering Town actually beat the Reds to it by sporting their shirt sponsor, 'Kettering Tyres' for a Southern League game in January 1976. Incidentally, the strip did not get another airing as the FA ordered the Poppies to remove the message from their shirts. They did continue to sport the legend 'Kettering T' for a few months as their then chief executive Derek Dougan claimed the 1972 FA ban on sponsorship had not been recorded in writing. However, the threat of a hefty fine brought to an end the non-leaguers' efforts. Liverpool unveiled their new 'name' home shirt a month before the start of the 79-80 season, Phil Thompson being pictured launching the shirt alongside a local beauty on the site of the current Clayton Square in Liverpool city centre. There are other claims related to shirt sponsor 'firsts'. Back in 1974 junior club Bellshill Athletic were apparently

1980-81 Away

sponsored by 'The Darby Inn' public house in the town. As far back as 1898, then champions Nottingham Forest apparently had a sponsor on their shirts in the form of 'Bovril'. Derby also lay claim to have had 'Saab' on their shirts ahead of the 1977-78 campaign — though as noted previously, the tops were never worn in competitive action, merely sported for promotional purposes.

1981-82 Home

1980-81 Home

NEW SPONSOR APPROACH

Coventry City attempted to break the mould of shirt sponsorship deals by incorporating the 'T' logo of the Talbot car company into their kit design in 1981. The proposal was also mooted to change the club's name to 'Coventry Talbot' — an idea that was banished almost as soon as it had first been unveiled.

However, the Sky Blues were subsequently boycotted by TV cameras until an alternative strip was released for televised games. The ban was lifted for the 1983-84 season.

1980-81 Keeper

1981-82 Home

1980 FA Cup S-F

1979-1982

1982-1983

Continued progress

1982-1983

1982-1983

82-83 PLAYERS Graeme Sharp, Kevin Sheedy, Adrian Heath
MANAGER Howard Kendall

ABOUT THE KIT

A V-neck design and white collarbone white piping replaced the previous shirt of four years. The traditional royal blue appeared a little less 'royal', while shirt 'technology' moved to more synthetic materials, the idea being that the modern man-made fibres would reduce 'moisture'. The white alternative kit from the previous season was introduced as the official away strip. Blue shorts with white trim were worn when colour clashes permitted — and likewise, blue socks replaced white. The all yellow strip became the third kit, being sported at West Brom with the design and trim of blue the same as that displayed on the white change kit. As previously, the Hafnia sponsor's logo was again only displayed for non-televised league matches.

1982-83 Home & keeper

1982–1983

ON-FIELD

Everton improved again to finish seventh in Division One, having lost only two home games and won six of their last eight league fixtures. They also reached the FA Cup quarter-finals, a run that included a victory over double-cup holders Tottenham Hotspur in round five at Goodison. But a late Frank Stapleton goal sent eventual winners Manchester United through 1-0 at Old Trafford. The League Cup again brought little joy, with Arsenal easing through 3-0 in round three at Highbury. Strangely, the Blues knocked Division Three club Newport County out of both competitions.

The youth team did provide some encouragement for the future though, reaching the FA Youth Cup final before losing out to Norwich City in a third game — this after the two-legged tie had ended 5-5 on aggregate.

Goals were shared around in the side, with Graeme Sharp (17), Kevin Sheedy, Andy King (both 13) and Adrian Heath (11) all reaching double figures.

1982-83 Away

OFF-FIELD

Neville Southall was one of several first-team players sent out on loan during the season. The Welshman would eventually return from Port Vale, win back the No 1 jersey from Jim Arnold, and go on to be the club's undisputed first choice goalkeeper until January 1997.

1982-83 Change shorts

1982-1983

RIVAL FIRM

Despite Umbro being club kit manufacturers, it did not stop rivals adidas muscling in. Here boss Howard Kendall sports a 'manager's coat', at Manchester United, in 1983.

STITCH IN TIME

Although the Umbro and Hafnia' logos were printed on the shirt, the gold club badge addition added a little bit of quality to the shirt.

DID YOU KNOW?

On-loan Blackburn defender Glenn Keeley was sent off 34 minutes into his Everton debut, becoming part of Merseyside derby folklore in the process. Liverpool ended up recording a 5-0 at Goodison Park.
The average crowd this season was less than 21,000 — the lowest since 1914-15. The following season would see a record post-war low of 19,343.

1983 All blue, FA Cup

SPONSORSHIP U-D

Speaking in the Everton v Coventry City programme from May 1983 (in a period of recession for the economy), then Blues secretary Jim Greenwood made the following comments related to the issue of shirt sponsorship:

"We feel that the television companies should concede this point, although it is probably true that, in the current climate, its value is not as high as three or four years ago. All companies have cut back on sponsorships and advertising budgets and the price for a shirt advertising deal, even with TV exposure, would not be as lucrative now. Nevertheless, it would provide a significant sum."

1982-83 Away, no sponsor

1983-1985
The sweet smell of success

1983-1985

KIT DESIGN **Le Coq Sportif** /// KIT SPONSOR **HAFNIA**

83-85 PLAYERS Andy Gray, Peter Reid, Derek Mountfield
MANAGER Howard Kendall

ABOUT THE KIT

French sportswear manufacturer Le Coq Sportif ('The Sporty Rooster') produced arguably the club's most famous home shirt — certainly since shirt sponsorship became the rule, rather than the exception. The company was founded in 1948 by Emile Camuset, the name deriving from the Gallic rooster. Chelsea, Tottenham, Aston Villa, Sunderland and Argentina's '86 World Cup winners sported their kits. They were amongst a host of companies who broke the Umbro/Bukta monopoly with adidas, Hummel, Nike and Patrick also muscling in.
The home shirt included a round-neck design with a V-neck white addition, while thin, darker blue stripes were designed within the material. A new badge design was also

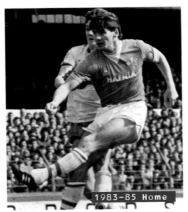

1983-85 Home

stiched into the material. Simple 'short' shorts included a blue stripe across the bottom of the shorts, while blue hoops ran across white socks.
The kit used new lightweight fabrics, with improvements in production allowing intricate designs to be woven or printed into the fabric.
The change strips saw Everton wear yellow (incorporating a

1983-85 Away

white V-neck) with blue or black shorts, and yellow or blue socks (variations dependent on clash with home club). A silver third kit (blue or black shorts and blue socks optional) was also introduced.
1983 saw TV companies relax their rules, allowing shirt sponsors to be broadcast. Sponsorship deals resultedly became more lucrative.

ON-FIELD

One of the most successful periods in the club's history, as the League, FA Cup, European Cup Winners' Cup and FA Charity Shield were won. From struggling near the foot of Division One at the end of 1983, an under-pressure Howard Kendall led Everton to seventh, the League Cup final and an FA Cup success — where Everton defeated Watford 2-0. The club's youngsters would also seal a second FA Youth Cup win.

It would prove a precursor to the Blues' most successful campaign — 1984-85. Having started off by beating Liverpool in the FA Charity Shield, a first league title in 15 years was won, the 90 First Division points accumulated being a record for the time. Although they were shocked by Grimsby Town in the League Cup, Everton reached the FA Cup and Cup Winners' Cup finals, both being reached after memorable semi-finals against Luton Town and Bayern Munich respectively. Rapid Vienna were beaten 3-1 to secure Everton's first-ever European trophy in Rotterdam,

1985 FA Cup final original

1983-85 Third

but the club's treble bid was ended three days later by Manchester United, 1-0 at Wembley after extra-time. The success of that team led to Everton being named World Team of the Year for 1985. Top scorers during the period were Adrian Heath (18) in 1983-84, and Graeme Sharp (30) the following campaign.

OFF-FIELD

Colin Harvey, who had returned in 1976 initially as part of the youth set-up, was promoted to first-team coach in 1983.

Neville Southall (Football Writers) and Peter Reid (PFA) took a clean sweep of the major player of the year awards in 1985.

FAMOUS MATCH
Everton 3-1 Bayern Munich (European Cup-Winners' Cup semi-final, second leg).

WRONG SHIRTS
Birmingham City kindly provided their away shirts — where Everton's lost in transit? — for a fixture at St Andrew's in January 1984. Everton went on to win 2-0.

KIT LOGOS
Football League restrictions meant shirt logos could only be a maximum of 81 square cm (32 square inches) — for TV games they had to be half this size.

DID YOU KNOW?
In the 1984 FA Cup final Kevin Richardson wore a different shirt. He had injured his arm in the League Cup semi-final against Aston Villa and his plaster-cast was deemed unsafe to wear with the bespoke short-sleeved blue shirts for the final, which had been embroidered with the match details. Richo had to make do with the standard home shirt from the season.

1983–85 Away

DID YOU KNOW?

The 1985 FA Cup final, as well as seeing United's Kevin Moran become the first man sent off in the fixture, was also the last Wembley attendance to top 100,000. Darren Oldroyd's two-minute sub appearance against Nottingham Forest in May 1985 is the shortest first-team career of any Everton player — a record that would be equalled nearly 22 years later.

Why Goodison hero wore a RED jersey

Pilkington Glass

EAGLE-EYED Evertonians spotted that goall was wearing a Doncaster Rovers jersey last S

THE MAN IN RED

Of course, our greatest-ever goalkeeper sported red in the 1985 European Cup Winners' Cup final, but it was not the first time — there was also another occasion earlier that season. Doncaster Rovers (including a young Ian Snodin) were the opposition at Goodison in the FA Cup, and with the Yorkshire side wearing an all-green strip (clashing with the colour of his usual top) — and Southall not too happy about the prospect of wearing a white jersey as he had done in a defeat at Norwich City, there was a simple switch to Doncaster's spare red top.

1984–85 Red

1984–85 Green

GREATEST EVER...

1983-85 Home

1984 FA Cup S-F Keeper

1984 FA Cup final

1984 League Cup S-F

1984 Le Coq Sportif: Chelsea v Everton

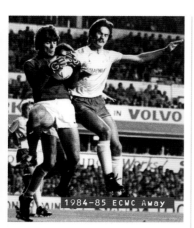

1984-85 ECWC Away

1983-85 Away

1984 FA Cup S-F

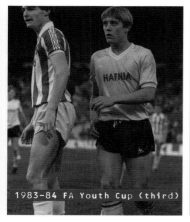

1983-84 FA Youth Cup (third)

1983-85 No 9 (Home)

1983-85 No 9 (Away)

1985-1986
It all ended in tears

1985-1986

85-86 PLAYERS Gary Lineker, Paul Bracewell, Pat van den Hauwe
MANAGER Howard Kendall

ABOUT THE KIT

Arguably the most radical change in the club's home design in the 20th century was the Everton 'bib'. The addition of white material covering the top area of the shirt — with yellow piping separating the white from the blue — was a step too far for many Everton traditionalists. First worn 'competitively' in the 1985 FA Charity Shield against Manchester United, it is the strip most associated with the 1986 FA Cup final defeat.

The away strip was basic yellow with the same-style blue V-neck and cuffs, with blue or yellow shorts worn with yellow socks. Japanese IT company NEC also began their 10-year association with the club.

1985-86 Home (TV sponsor)

1985-86 Home (non-TV sponsor)

ON-FIELD

A 2-0 FA Charity Shield defeat of Manchester United ensured an element of revenge for the Blues following their FA Cup final defeat a few months before. Unfortunately, the campaign as a whole will be remembered as a case of what might have been. League Cup ambitions had ended by the time Howard Kendall's side built a strong challenge for the league and cup double. But a late-season league defeat (only the second in 1986) at Oxford United all but ended title hopes, with Liverpool's late winning run overhauling the Blues. Kenny Dalglish's side also defeated Everton 3-1 in the first-ever all-Merseyside FA Cup final, after the Toffees had led at the break through Gary Lineker – the 40th of a memorable one-season campaign.

1985-86 Away

1985-86 Away (non-TV sponsor)

1985-86 Away (TV sponsor)

OFF-FIELD

With English clubs banned from European competition, those teams who would have been in Continental action the following campaign played in the Screen Sports Super Cup, a competition devised in part to help clubs make up the shortfall in revenue. Everton would qualify for the two-legged final – although this would be played the following season, against Liverpool. A dispute over TV rights meant the first half of the season was only witnessed by match-goers.

Gary Lineker won both the PFA and the Football Writers' Player of the Year awards.

FAMOUS MATCH
Liverpool 0-2 Everton
(Division One).

CUP FINAL TRACKIES

Arguably the final act by Le Coq Sportif, these traditional tracksuits were worn on the return journey by the squad following the 1986 FA Cup final.

BIB LOGOS

The 1986 final shirt, complete with 'FA CUP FINAL WEMBLEY 1986' text. Note too the 'smaller' NEC sponsor, due to TV coverage restrictions.

DID YOU KNOW?

Manchester United won their first 10 league games – but faltered, finishing fourth. October 1985 at Chelsea saw Kevin Ratcliffe forced to take over in goal when Neville Southall was sent off – the last time a Blues' outfielder has done this. Future Everton striker Tony Cottee won the PFA Young Player of the Year award due to his goalscoring performances for West Ham.

1985-86 Keeper (green)

1985-86 Away shorts

MERSEYSIDE UNITES

It was early 1986 when the decision was made for Everton and Liverpool players to line up for this special team photo. It was produced by the Prudential Assurance Company, in a bid to promote the image of football on Merseyside. The logistics of getting the squads together wasn't easy, as neither side wanted to go to the other's training ground! Stalemate ensued until the Reds reluctantly agreed to make the short journey to Everton's now former Bellefield training headquarters.

1986-1989

1986-1989
Champions in all blue

1986-1989

86-89 PLAYERS Neville Southall, Kevin Ratcliffe, Trevor Steven
MANAGERS Howard Kendall, Colin Harvey

ABOUT THE KIT

A return to Umbro brought blue socks back to the home strip. In what became a recurring theme, Everton's kits were often replicated at other clubs. The diamond shadow effect in the shirt, the simple V-neck, square-pattern shorts, diamond design in one corner of said shorts plus white turn-ups on the socks – it was almost a carbon-copy of Nottingham Forest's 1986/87 design.

It is the last time the club kept the same home strip for three seasons, and by the last campaign the deep royal blue showed signs of fading towards a lighter blue/purple hue.

An almost exact design was produced in yellow and blue for the away strip, while a third kit (never worn competitively) was all-white.

The 1988-89 season saw yellow retained, although plain yellow shorts with simple Umbro logo were worn at Coventry City – along with yellow socks with a blue Umbro diamond design on the turn-ups. The third kit was grey and white striped, with a button-down collar used for the first time on an Everton shirt. Blue lettering and collar trim were other additions, while the blue shorts with white and grey side diamond pattern were usually worn with white socks, incorporating blue Umbro diamond turn-ups.

1986-87 Forest v Everton

1986-87 Home

1988-89 Home (faded)

ON-FIELD

Having begun the period by holding Double winners Liverpool to a 1-1 draw in the FA Charity Shield, injury ravaged Everton regained the Division One crown, the club's ninth and last championship to date. The winning margin was nine points ahead of Liverpool, with the club's home record of 16 wins and one defeat in 21 the key to the success. Disappointingly, defeat to Wimbledon in round five of the FA Cup was the Blues' first defeat in the competition, excluding at Wembley, for four years. There were also defeats to Liverpool in the League Cup quarter-final, and the Screen Sports Super Cup final. Colin Harvey's reign began with silverware in the form of the FA Charity Shield, FA Cup winners Coventry City losing 1-0. But the champions could only finish fourth in the league, while in the cups a League Cup semi-final and run to the last 16 of the FA Cup — which included eight ties due to replays — was the sum total from 1987-88. Rebuilding ahead of 1988-89

1986-88 Away (blue shorts)

saw Everton installed as one of the favourites to land the league, but the mix of old and new failed to blend. The Blues finished eighth, their lowest placing for seven years. They did reach the finals of the FA Cup and Simod Cup, but lost both in extra-time, to Liverpool and Nottingham Forest respectively.

1988-89 Goalkeeper

OFF-FIELD

Assistant-manager Colin Harvey took over the hot seat vacated by Athletic Bilbao-bound Howard Kendall in the summer of 1987.
Everton broke the British transfer record to sign Tony Cottee for £2.2m in the summer of 1988. It was a club record fee that stood for over six years.

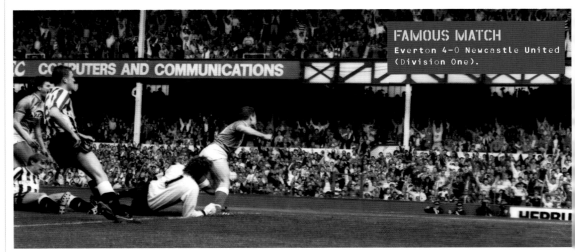

FAMOUS MATCH
Everton 4-0 Newcastle United
(Division One).

CHANGE SOCKS

White socks with blue turn-ups
(left) were worn as
alternatives with the blue
strip, certainly in 1986-87.
The yellow? Worn with the grey
and white third kit, in 88-89.

DIAMOND NUMBERS

The kit manufacturers' logo
was first introduced on EFC
numbers by Le Coq Sportif, and
Umbro continued the tradition
of extra 'product' placement.

DID YOU KNOW?

Tony Cottee scored 34
seconds into his Everton bow,
going on to complete a
hat-trick against Newcastle
United in August 1988. He
would finish his Goodison
career six years and 99 goals
later.
Stuart McCall became the
first player to score twice
as a sub in an FA Cup final in
1989 — Liverpool's Ian Rush
would repeat the feat in the
same game.

1988-89 All blue

1988-90 Third

UMBRO MEN

Everton went back to Wembley last week – covered in diamonds! Yes, the famous diamond logo of Umbro is back on our kit after a gap of four years.

The new strip – modelled here by World Cup quartet Trevor Steven, Gary Stevens, Peter Reid and Graeme Sharp – allies the classical look and traditional Royal Blue with innovative styling and fabric technology, the jersey featuring a unique diamond shadow effect in a shiny and matt finish.

The new agreement also means that Umbro supply tracksuits and training gear as well as extensive package of off-the-field leisurewear to ensure players are both comfortable and projecting a total team image when travelling to away games.

Manager Howard Kendall says: "We were very conscious that our fans were anxious for us to return to a kit more in keeping with Everton's traditional look".

Replica kits will be available in the Souvenir Shop – and every sale will be a boost for Merseyside's economy. The replica kits are produced locally at Umbro's factory in Ellesmere Port.

1989 FA CUP FINAL

The Wembley showpiece was played only weeks after the Hillsborough disaster, which saw 96 Liverpool fans lose their lives at their semi-final tie against Nottingham Forest. An emotional final saw Everton hit back twice, the first time in the last minute of normal time, before losing 3-2 after extra-time. The Blues also wore a new strip — the club's new 1989-91 home kit.

KIT LAUNCH 1986

Everton reverted to Umbro as their official kit supplier after three years with Le Coq Sportif.

In the official programme for the first league match of the 1986-87 season, against Nottingham Forest, manager Howard Kendall's comment was: "We were very conscious that our fans were anxious for us to return to a kit more in keeping with Everton's traditional look."

An additional note from the piece read:

'Every sale will be a boost for Merseyside's economy. The replica kits are produced locally at Umbro's factory in Ellesmere Port.'

1989 FA Cup final

1988-1990

The Daily Telegraph

BARCLAYS BANK

1989-1991
Transitional phase

1989-1991

KIT DESIGN Umbro /// KIT SPONSOR NEC

89-91 PLAYERS Tony Cottee, Stuart McCall, Norman Whiteside
MANAGERS Colin Harvey, Jimmy Gabriel (caretaker), Howard Kendall

ABOUT THE KIT

The new home kit, first worn in the '89 FA Cup final, would also be a decision repeated in 1995 when another new Umbro strip was sported for the first time. Used over the next two seasons, subtle changes over those two campaigns included clearer numbering — and the addition of the Football League badge logos on the arms. A button-down collar was also added to the home shirt for the first time — replicating 'technology' used on the grey and white third shirt.

Blue and grey patches were sewn on each side of the shorts, and a chequered flag-style white square design was produced within the sock turn-ups. While the grey and white-striped third kit was retained, two yellow change strips were worn during this period. An all yellow strip with blue touches

1989-91 Home

replacing the white on the home strip was worn on occasions — including two FA Cup replays at Oldham Athletic during 1989-90. The following season, a new yellow and blue away strip was introduced. A prominent blue zig-zag line across the shirt was a big feature, along with flash shapes within the material. Lined blue triangles were also a feature, similarly in yellow on the sides of the blue shorts. The yellow socks changed little, with blue diamonds on the turn-ups. Chelsea, also on Umbro's books, would also wear a similar strip.

1990-91 Home

1989-1991

ON-FIELD

Despite topping the table early in 1989-90, a mid-season wobble ensured a sixth-place finish. Three away games were won, although only two lost at home. In the FA Cup, Everton played seven games before going out to Oldham in a fifth-round, second replay, while there was League Cup disappointment at Nottingham Forest — the late winner coming via an indirect free-kick after Neville Southall had been deemed to be holding onto the ball for too long. The following season began with Colin Harvey residing over a run of only one league win in 10 games before the axe came, after a League Cup defeat at Sheffield United. Howard Kendall returned, steadying the ship before securing 11th courtesy of a run of unbeaten games at the back-end of the campaign. The FA Cup saw defeat to West Ham in the quarter-final, after Liverpool had been seen off in round five, while an unexpected Wembley appearance came in the Zenith Data Systems Cup — Crystal Palace winning 4-1 aet.

1990-92 Away original

1990-92 Numbers

1989-90 Numbers

OFF-FIELD

Howard Kendall returned to the club for a second time in November 1990, replacing Colin Harvey — who returned as his assistant. In the interim coach Jimmy Gabriel had taken charge for one game — a 3-0 victory over QPR, only the Blues' second league success of 1990-91.

1989-90 Third

1989-1991

FOOTBALL LEAGUE

The official logo became
compulsory on each shirt arm
from the 1990-91 season. It
would last two campaigns
before the beginning of the FA
Premier League in 92-93.

EVERTON LOGOS

This is the last version of
the official club crest on the
shirt. Future shirts would
include this crest — but
simplified on the shield
background.

DID YOU KNOW?

Ray Atteveld and Stefan
Rehn, signed in the summer of
1989, were amongst the first
overseas players to
represent the club.
Due to subsequent rule
changes, the three-game epic
against Liverpool in the 1991
FA Cup — which included a
memorable 4-4 draw after
extra-time at Goodison Park
— is the last time a tie has
been won in England in the
third match.

1989-90 Away

1990-91 All blue

1989-90 Keeper — red

CHANGES

With all blue and all yellow kits being worn away from Goodison, the period also saw the goalkeeper's jersey become an added commercial bonus for Umbro. Neville Southall sported two different green shirts during these seasons, while a predominantly red top was also worn as a change version in pre-season games in the summer of 1989.

The Oldham v Everton FA Cup replays at Boundary Park in 1990 showcased two Umbro sides — and another similarity between both team's home kits.

1989-90 Keeper

1990-91 Keeper

1990 Umbro v Umbro

ATLANTIC
COMMUNICATIONS
Hutchison
Telecom
Everton Club
Carlsberg
PREMIER LEAGUE

merseymart
051 734 4000

1991-1993
Whole new ball game?

1991-1993

91-93 PLAYERS Peter Beardsley, Martin Keown, Dave Watson
MANAGER Howard Kendall

ABOUT THE KIT

Some 1990s graphics and a neat white button-down collar with blue piping were incorporated into the new home shirt. A white efc logo on one arm was an added addition. The logo was copied in blue on the white shorts, the kit completed by blue socks with white turn-ups. Manufacturers began to create designs aimed at the fashion market — or to ensure shirts 'went' with jeans.

The shirts during 1992-93 began to include new logos. NEC's new design saw the letters being more rounded (from January 1993) — while Umbro's lettering changed from lower case to upper.

A controversial new away kit replaced the yellow and blue strip for 1992-93. Salmon pink and dark blue stripes were introduced, in salute of what was assumed to be Everton's

1991-93 Replica Home

Late 1992 Home

first kit when they moved to Goodison 100 years before. Mixed feelings from fans in the early days of the kits' release were only enhanced when some shirts were printed with the club's Latin nickname being wrongly printed on the badge as: 'Nil Satis Nisi Optimun'. Predominantly blue shorts —

1991-92 Home

March 1993 Home

although salmon pink were also worn — and salmon pink socks completed the kit.

A third kit was also rushed out in 92-93, worn at Crystal Palace and Aston Villa, of white shirt, blue change shorts or the home white shorts, and white socks. This shirt also included the old NEC and Umbro lettering.

ON-FIELD

The 1991-92 season was the last old Division One campaign, before the FA Premier League came into being for 92-93.
Unfortunately, the Blues did not distinguish themselves in either season, with inconsistency dogging the team despite the general brilliance of Peter Beardsley. The Blues finished 12th and 13th respectively, with Beardsley — who scored 20 goals — and Neville Southall ever presents in 91-92.
The cup competitions brought little joy, with the last 16 of the League Cup being the longest run Everton enjoyed — in both campaigns.
Apart from Beardsley, Tony Cottee was the only other player to reach double figures in the goalscoring charts in both seasons.

1992-93 Third

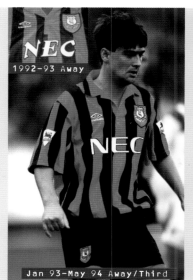

1992-93 Away

Jan 93-May 94 Away/Third

1992-93 Third, home shorts

OFF-FIELD

The start of the 1991-92 season heralded the first time the Lower Gwladys Street had been made all-seated. Everton, Aston Villa and Blackburn Rovers became the only clubs to be founder members of both the Football League, in 1888, and the Premier League, in 1992.

Goalkeepers were allowed to be named as one of three substitutes for the first time, in 1992.
The attendance of 3,039 for the Wimbledon v Everton match at Selhurst Park in 1993 is the lowest top-flight attendance since the Second World War.

1991-1993

UMBRO HALVES

A full logo on each number, plus a tasteful diamond half in the top right-hand corner ensured the manufacturer received full recognition on the back of the club's shirts.

KIT LOGOS

An 'efc' graphic was not the only addition to the new home shirt. As well as the FA Premier League logo replacing the Football League version in 1992, the club badge was updated with a shield design.

DID YOU KNOW?

Debutant Barry Horne scored Everton's first goal in the FA Premier League.

The 1992-93 season is only the third time the Blues have won away from home (eight matches) more times than at Goodison (seven). It happened for a fourth time in 2008-09.

The 5-2 win at Man City in May 1993 saw sub keepers Andy Dibble (City) and Jason Kearton make appearances.

1991-1993

1991-92 White socks

1991-92 Keeper

1992-93 Keeper

DO WE LIKE ORANGE?

A league fixture at Luton Town in 1991-92 saw Everton forced to don the orange change shirts of the opposition. The referee had apparently deemed the Blues' usual home shirt as clashing with the Hatters' usual top — there being too much blue on the white Luton shirt for the officials' liking. Having travelled south without their usual yellow change strip, Howard Kendall's team were forced to borrow from the hosts. The shirt would prove a lucky omen though, as substitute Robert Warzycha's second-half effort secured a 1-0 victory, ending a run of two successive league defeats.

1991-92 All blue

Luton v Everton, November 1991

1993-1995
Rollercoaster ride

1993 - 1995

1993-1995

93-95 PLAYERS Paul Rideout, Barry Horne, Andy Hinchcliffe
MANAGERS Howard Kendall, Jimmy Gabriel (caretaker), Mike Walker, Joe Royle

ABOUT THE KIT

Shiny Everton crests and an Umbro diamond were included within the fabric of the new home shirt. There were several other 'innovations' on the shirt, the white buttonless collar with blue trim being the most sober of them. The tower crest from the Everton badge was added just below the collar, on suede-like material. The club badge became more prominent within a shield, while a white and thin black band around each arm included an Everton tag on each. Another Umbro tag on one side, and an 'official product' transfer on the bottom corner, completed the shirt. White shorts included blue banding on waist and legs, while the socks reverted to white for the first time since 85-86, which incorporated blue turn-ups and white diamonds.

1995 FA Cup SF

Blue shorts and/or socks were also worn with the home shirt when a colour clash occurred. The salmon pink and blue kit was retained, and a white and blue third kit was introduced. A white shirt with white button collar, incorporated dark blue piping. Dark blue shorts with a white strip on the legs, and dark blue socks with white turn-ups completed the strip.

1993-95 All blue

The two change strips were replaced by a new white and black kit ahead of 94-95, the white shirt with black button collar incorporating a design down either side. The look suggests that a tractor — with grey painted tyres — has driven over the shirt. Black shorts sported this design on either side, while the black socks included white Umbro turn-ups.

ON-FIELD

1993-94 season saw the Blues
survive relegation — just.
Everton had topped the table
after three wins from three.
But by early January 1994,
with Mike Walker as new boss,
the team was in freefall.
Walker's first league game
brought a 6-2 win over
Swindon, but an FA Cup exit to
Bolton — having led 2-0 —
followed. Three league wins in
15 left the club in the drop
zone on the final day. Needing
to beat Wimbledon, they won
3-2, having trailed 2-0.
Lessons didn't appear to have
been learnt in 1994-95. It was
Everton's worst start to a
league season, the Blues
taking 13 games before
winning. But once Walker was
axed, replaced by Joe Royle,
form returned. Backed up by
defensive organisation, a
'Dogs of War' midfield, Andy
Hinchcliffe's set-piece
delivery and the forward
menace of Paul Rideout and
Duncan Ferguson, the Blues
recovered to finish 15th. They
also won the FA Cup, beating
Manchester United 1-0 after a
memorable semi-final defeat
of Spurs, 4-1 at Elland Road.

1993-94 Third

1994-95 Original away

OFF-FIELD

Howard Kendall resigned in
December 1993, in the wake of
a 1-0 win over Southampton. A
dispute with the board, having
been denied the funds to
purchase Dion Dublin from
Manchester United, proved the
clincher for the manager.
Jimmy Gabriel took over as
caretaker, although the Blues
did not record a win before

Norwich City boss Mike Walker
took over in January 1994.
His record proved dismal,
winning just six of 35 games,
nearly relegating the club
before Joe Royle took over
that November.
Goodison became all-seater
with the completion of the
new Park End stand for the
start of the 1994-95 season.

1993-1995

1993-95 Home

NAME BRAND

1993-94 was the first season players were assigned a shirt number and name, printed on the back. The No 13 is from the season before, 1992-93.

KIT TAGS

Tags proved a popular addition to the home shirt, with these sleeve ones complemented by an Umbro tag displayed on one side of the shirt.

DID YOU KNOW?

A 2-0 win at Southampton in August 1993 was the first game Everton players wore their name and squad number on the back of their shirts. Beagrie (No 11) and Ebbrell (14) were the scorers.
The Blues kept a record seven successive clean sheets between November and December 1994.
The 1994-95 campaign is the last time the top flight consisted of 22 teams.

1993-1995

1995 FA Cup final strip

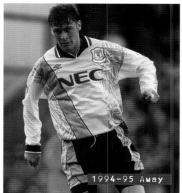

1994-95 Away

NEV IN BLACK?

It was claimed that Neville Southall deliberately asked for a black goalkeeping kit, when worn between 1992-1994. The belief was that it enabled him to blend in with the crowd behind the goal — and thereby take strikers by surprise. However, the veteran keeper would wear a succession of shirts during this era which seemed to belie this notion. These included this green and 'psychedelic' number (below) — and the banana yellow and black strip sported in the 1995 FA Cup final.

CUP FINAL FASHION

Umbro took the opportunity to unveil the club's new home strip for the 1995 FA Cup final. A change from mainly white socks to blue and black hoops was the main difference, with black trim also being utilised on the shirt collar and on the sides of the shorts. The shirt reverted to tagless, while there was a more sober pattern within the fabric, and a blue and white ribbed collar. The match was also significant as being the last game the players sported 'NEC' on their shirts, as the company called time on their 10-year sponsorship.

1992-94 Keeper

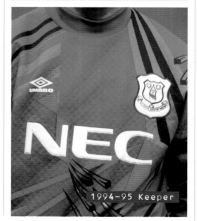

1994-95 Keeper

1993-1995

1995·1997
Europe dashed, Royle end

1995-1997

95-97 PLAYERS Andrei Kanchelskis, Duncan Ferguson, Graham Stuart
MANAGERS Joe Royle, Dave Watson (caretaker)

ABOUT THE KIT

First worn at Wembley in May 1995, the only change in the new home shirts for the 1995-96 season was in the shirt sponsor, `Danka´ replacing long-time partners NEC. Limited edition sponsorless shirts had been produced by Umbro for the final, the news being widely reported during the period that a new shirt sponsor would be adorning the shirt come the following season. The trend for longer shorts was the other noticeable difference from previous Everton strips.
The `tractor´ strip remained in place for 1995-96 too, again with the new shirt sponsors receiving pride of place. 1996-97 saw the club revert to yellow and black stripes, the black areas on the top half of the shirt incorporating what

1995-97 Original home

looked like a brushing of blue paint. A more solid V-neck collar was added, in light of criticisms of the collar on the home shirt. Umbro also introduced their new logo — a simple upper case text, and no diamond logo for the first time since the sportswear manufacturer took over from Le Coq Sportif in 1986. The mainly black shorts were also made baggier. Socks were yellow with black turn-ups.

1995-97 Home

1995-1997

ON-FIELD

Everton began 1995-96 by seeing off Blackburn to win the FA Charity Shield. But by Christmas, the Blues were in mid-table and out of the European Cup Winners' and League Cups. From then, despite FA Cup embarrassment at Port Vale, the team lost just three league games, inspired by 16-goal Andrei Kanchelskis. Needing victory over Aston Villa on the final day, and an Arsenal failure to beat Bolton to qualify for the UEFA Cup, the Blues won 1-0. But a late goal gave the Gunners a 2-1 win, leaving Everton in sixth.

There were mixed results in the first half of 1996-97, but a win at Derby in December saw the Blues touted as title dark horses. They would win only three more league games, including a club record-equalling six successive defeats. FA Cup defeat to Bradford was almost as humbling as League Cup woe v York. Joe Royle's departure, in part due to poor form, saw a threadbare squad limp on to survive the drop, eventually by only two points in 15th.

1995-96 Away

1996-97 Original away

OFF-FIELD

The Blues broke their transfer record twice during the period. Andrei Kanchelskis was signed for £5m from Manchester United in August 1995, while Nick Barmby joined for £5.75m from Middlesbrough 14 months later. The 7-1 victory over Southampton in November 1996 is a Premier League best for the club — a mark equalled 11 years later.

Joe Royle quit in 1997, stepping down ahead of the March transfer deadline having been blocked from bringing in three players, including Barry Horne as player-coach. Dave Watson was made caretaker for the remainder of the campaign.

1995-1997

SHODDY MATERIAL

The fabric of Duncan Ferguson's shirt fails to survive the full 90 minutes against Tottenham in 1997.

CLUB SHIELDS

The 'tractor tyre' white away shirt, released in the summer of 1994, was the first to utilise the shield design. The new home kit the following year followed the trend.

DID YOU KNOW?

Graham Stuart enjoyed his best-ever goalscoring season in 1995-96, netting 14 goals. Andrei Kanchelskis joined Fiorentina for a then club record £8m in early 1997. Neville Southall was dropped for the first time in 15 years, at Newcastle in 1997. Tore Andre Flo, Claus Eftevaag and Barry Horne were reportedly the men Joe Royle was refused the chance to sign when he resigned.

1995-1997

1995-97 Home numbers

1996-97 Away

1996-97 Home

VARIATIONS?

An eye-watering illuminous orange, with black and yellow 'patterns' was the goalkeeping jersey of choice in 1996-97. Neville Southall sported the yellow and black from the 1995 FA Cup final for much of 1995-96 — but the orange made that design seem almost timid in comparison. Worn sporting two different styles of shirt sponsorship, generally with black shorts and socks, the strip also highlighted Umbro's 'make-do' policy. The picture (left), of an Everton goal v Nottingham Forest, shows keeper Mark Crossley wearing a familiar offering — Forest were also on Umbro's books.

1996-97 Keeper

1996-97 Keeper

1995-96 Keeper

1997-1999

Relegation scrapes

1997-1999

KIT DESIGN Umbro /// KIT SPONSOR One2One

97-99 PLAYERS Gary Speed, Olivier Dacourt, Thomas Myhre
MANAGERS Howard Kendall, Walter Smith

1997-99 Original home

July 1997 / July 1997

GRANT 20 1996-97

GERRARD 13 1997-98

ABOUT THE KIT

A late unveiling ahead of 97-98
(Dave Watson's testimonial saw
the club wearing the old strip
with temporary sponsor — see
pic far right), there were some
notable changes — not least in
the return to white socks. A
1970s-style filled in white V-
neck with white collar was a
notable addition (along with an
'Everton' band), as was the
multi-coloured chest 'strip'
behind the new shirt sponsor,
mobile phone company 'One2One'.
A first for the home shirt, a
similar shirt addition had been
sported in the late 1950s/early
60s on a white away shirt. There
was Umbro diamond trim on the
end of each sleeve, with
additional yellow piping, while
the badge was encased in a
round patch. The blue was less
'royal' than previous years,
and there was the inclusion of
logos proclaiming shirt

technology such as 'Vapa Tech'.
Plain white shorts displayed a
blue and yellow band on the
legs, while change blue shorts
and socks were worn in some
away games.

The yellow away kit — complete
with new shirt sponsor — was
retained for 1997-98, but 98-99
saw new white and yellow strips
introduced, both including a
more prominent sponsors' logo.

The white strip, worn with blue
or white shorts and white socks,
included retro-style Umbro
diamonds on the sleeves. The
yellow strip, worn with black or
yellow shorts and yellow socks,
was a plainer affair — the
diamonds, like on the white
kits' shorts, retained on the
sides. Incidentally, Premier
League standardised numbers
were introduced in 1997-98.

1997-1999

ON-FIELD

Howard Kendall's appointment, for a third spell, ended months of uncertainty. But beyond Slaven Bilic, little of real quality was brought in. Despite some encouraging results, a 4-0 defeat at new champions Arsenal left Everton going into the final day at home to Coventry needing a better result than Bolton — who were at Chelsea — to stay up. An unlikely Gareth Farrelly screamer, a missed Nick Barmby pen and a weak headed Dion Dublin equaliser ensured a 1-1 draw — but fortunately the London Blues won 2-0 to ensure Everton survival on goal difference. There was some silverware though, in the form of the FA Youth Cup.

Walter Smith replaced Kendall and real money was spent for 1998-99. But again struggle ensued, with lack of goals a problem. The forced sale of Duncan Ferguson helped little, and by Easter — soon after FA Cup quarter-final defeat at Newcastle — the Blues were in the drop zone. But new-boy Kevin Campbell's goals helped banish relegation fears.

1998-99 Original away

1998-99 Replica third

OFF-FIELD

After a fruitless search for a new manager, including approaches to Bobby Robson and Andy Gray, Howard Kendall returned for a third spell in June 1997 from Sheffield United. His tenure lasted just one season as the club again came close to losing their top-division status.

Walter Smith was subsequently appointed as new boss in the summer of '98.

Danka ended their two-season shirt sponsorship of the club in '97 when the company decided to focus on F1. Mobile phone operator One2One replaced them, beginning a five-year association with the club.

1997-1999

1997-98 Kit launch

TECHNOLOGY?

Apparent advances in science
saw Umbro introduce 'Vapa
Tech' fabric on many football
shirts during the period —
presumably to help the wearer
keep cool and reduce
'moisture management'.

SHIRT LOGO

As well as gloryfying in new
technology, Umbro also added
this patch to the home shirt
— the mention of Goodison
Park on an Everton shirt was
possibly a first, though.

DID YOU KNOW?

Club appearance record
holder Neville Southall
played the last of his 751
first-team games against
Tottenham Hotspur in
November 1997.
Everton's first league goal
at Goodison Park in 1998-99
came at the end of October.
The overall tally was a
meagre three goals in 12
games until mid-February,
when the Blues beat
Middlesbrough 5-0.

1997-98 Keeper

1997-98 Away

1997-98 Keeper

1998-99 Third (Back)

1998-2000 Keeper

1997-99 All blue

CLUB COLOURS

A variety of goalkeeping colours were adorned during the period, with the 1996-97 orange number being phased out during 97-98. A lime green and black creation was a common outfit, while the following season a light and dark green shirt and shorts combination, often worn with white socks, became the norm. Outfield strips included the 1996-97 yellow (with new sponsor for 97-98); a yellow third kit — the unusual 'Umbro' lettering on the back of the shirt pictured left; the all blue home 'away' strip (left, bottom); and a neat white and blue away (below).

1998-99 Away

1999-2000

Improving blues

1999-2000

KIT DESIGN Umbro, Puma /// **KIT SPONSOR** One2One

99-00 PLAYERS Kevin Campbell, Nick Barmby, John Collins
MANAGER Walter Smith

ABOUT THE KIT

Introduced at the tale end of the 1998-99 season, the new home strip was warmly received by fans, with a return to royal blue being a big plus. An unusual white V-neck collar — the material was 'bigger' near the shoulders — a return to the Umbro logo, white cuffs and white piping were other touches on the shirt. Plain white shorts with blue piping (blue, with white piping an alternative away from home), and another return to blue socks with white trim on the turn-ups made up the kit, in what would prove to be Umbro's last home strip for the club for four seasons.
The 2000-01 new Puma strip was actually worn on the final day of 1999-00, in a disappointing home defeat to Middlesbrough. The white away kit from the previous season was sported as a third strip, while a new all

1999-2000 Original home

yellow away kit was introduced. Minimilist in style, a black round-neck collar and black piping patterns on the arms and sides of the shorts were the main touches of note.

1999-2000 Launch

ON-FIELD

An improvement on some of the performances of the late 1990s, Everton's 13th-place finish was the club's best in four years. A failure to record a victory in their last four games cost the Blues a top-10 finish, in a season that showed some encouraging signs for the future.

Victory at Anfield is the last time the club have won at their former ground, ahead of the 2009-10 campaign. Four goals or more were also scored in seven league games, an unusually freescoring statistic under Walter Smith. There was an embarrassing draw at Exeter City in the FA Cup, the last of nine winless league and cup games although the Blues eventually reached the last eight, before going out to Aston Villa 2-1. The League Cup also saw a weakened side knocked out by Oxford United 2-1 on aggregate in round two. Kevin Campbell finished as top scorer with 12 goals, while there were also notable contributions from Nick Barmby (10), David Unsworth (9) and Joe-Max Moore (8).

1999-2000 Original third

OFF-FIELD

Bill Kenwright took control of the club from Peter Johnson in December 1999 — the Blues celebrating with a 5-0 victory over Sunderland.

Dave Watson made the final appearance of his glittering Everton career in January 2000 against Tottenham Hotspur. Having stayed on the club staff, he left to manage Tranmere Rovers in summer 2001.

Puma would become Everton's new kit manufacturer from the 2000-01 campaign. They were allowed to give fans a sneak preview when the team sported the strip in the final game of 1999-00.

FAMOUS MATCH
Liverpool 0-1 Everton
(Premier League).

NEW TREND

Wearing the new kit in the last home match of the previous season. The 1999-00 strip was sported for the final home game of 98-99, a 6-0 win over West Ham. It was also worn at Southampton in the final game a week later.

ADDED NUMBER

The first instance of a players' number being sported on Everton shorts occurred on the official home strip during the campaign.

DID YOU KNOW?

Richard Gough became the club's oldest goalscorer in the Premier League, age **37** and **138** days, after netting a header in a 4-1 defeat of Southampton in August 1999. Everton's last game of the 20th century yielded a 0-0 draw at Bradford City on December 28.

The 4-0 win at West Ham United in February 2000 is the club's best in the Premier League era.

1999-2000 Third

1999-2000 Away

GREEN OR YELLOW?

The goalkeeper strip for 1999-00 varied, with the green strip from 1998-99 being more commonly sported.
A bright yellow effort, with black trim, was also introduced, as signified by Umbro's reintroduction of the diamond logo. The kit was completed with black shorts and white socks.

1999-2000 Keeper yellow

1999-2000 All blue

May 2000 New Puma home

1999-2000

2000-2002
21st century changes

2000-2002

00-02 PLAYERS David Weir, David Unsworth, Scot Gemmill
MANAGERS Walter Smith, David Moyes

ABOUT THE KIT

This period is the last time the club have kept the same home strip for two seasons, the unofficial club policy being altered to celebrate the club competing in 100 years of top-flight football.

Everton's first-ever Puma kit was unveiled at the end of 1999-00 season. A more silky fabric and slightly paler than the previous incarnation (it was unkindly dubbed as being too similar to Birmingham City's strip), other features included white side panels, the new club badge and polo shirt-style buttonless collar. There was little variation in shorts design, while the sock turn-ups were white.

Four away kits, plus five goalkeeping strips were worn during these years. A simple yellow and blue and a white, blue and black third kit were introduced in 2000-01 — although the latter, with a band across the shirt reminscent of the late 50s/early 60s away top, was rarely used, if at all. Two more were brought in for 2001-02 — a grey and black away strip, the shirt incorporating a V-neck design. There was also a salmon pink and black third kit, worn unsuccessfully once, at Blackburn Rovers.

2000-02 Original blue

2000-02 All blue

2000-01 Away

ON-FIELD

The period saw the Blues back in the relegation mire — with 16th and 15th finishes only hinting at the struggles. 2000-01 saw embarrassing cup exits to Bristol Rovers and Tranmere Rovers and very mixed form, which included a home win over runners-up Arsenal and a 5-0 defeat at Manchester City — who were relegated that season. Survival was only guaranteed in the third-to-last game of the season, a 2-1 victory over Bradford City — who actually missed two penalties in the match. Kevin Campbell was top scorer with 10 goals.

An encouraging start to 01-02 soon evaporated, and having been knocked out on pens by Crystal Palace in the League Cup, it was a run in the FA Cup that appeared to keep Walter Smith at the helm. Having won only one league game in 13 matches since mid-December, a woeful 3-0 defeat at Middlesbrough in the quarter-finals signalled the end in mid-March — and the appointment of David Moyes. Four wins and one draw in nine games were enough to survive.

2001-02 Original away

2000-01 Third

OFF-FIELD

David Moyes became the 13th person to manage Everton after leaving Preston in March 2002. His first game, a 2-1 win over Fulham, saw David Unsworth open the scoring after only 32 seconds. One2One ended their shirt sponsorship at the end of the 2001-02 season.

2001-02 Third

2001-02 Away Launch

PREMIER NUMBERS

1980s names...in the 21st century. Former players of the mid-80s glory days were presented with shirts from the modern era at a celebratory dinner.

NEW LABEL

A fresh addition by Puma, 'authentication' tags have become something of a normal addition to shirts. This label is taken from the 2000-01 away shirt.

DID YOU KNOW?

The club's Reserves won the FA Premier League Northern Section in 2001.

The £8m received from Arsenal for Francis Jeffers in June 2001 equalled the biggest fee ever received by the club.

Everton's youngsters, inspired by a certain Wayne Rooney, reached the final of the FA Youth Cup in 2002, losing to Aston Villa 4-2 on aggregate.

2000-01 Keeper orange

2001-02 Keeper white

ALL THE COLOURS

Orange? Sky blue? Black? White? Green? The No 1 position during the period saw Steve Simonsen, Paul Gerrard and Thomas Myhre share goalkeeping duties, with the three failing to really establish themselves. Surely the wealth of kits on offer can't have helped. Indeed, at Newcastle in April 2002, a hastily put together green version was introduced, the usual kits clashing with the home side. It did little to bring the Blues luck — as the Magpies ran out 6-2 winners.

2000-01 Keeper blue

2001-02 Keeper black

2001-02 Keeper green

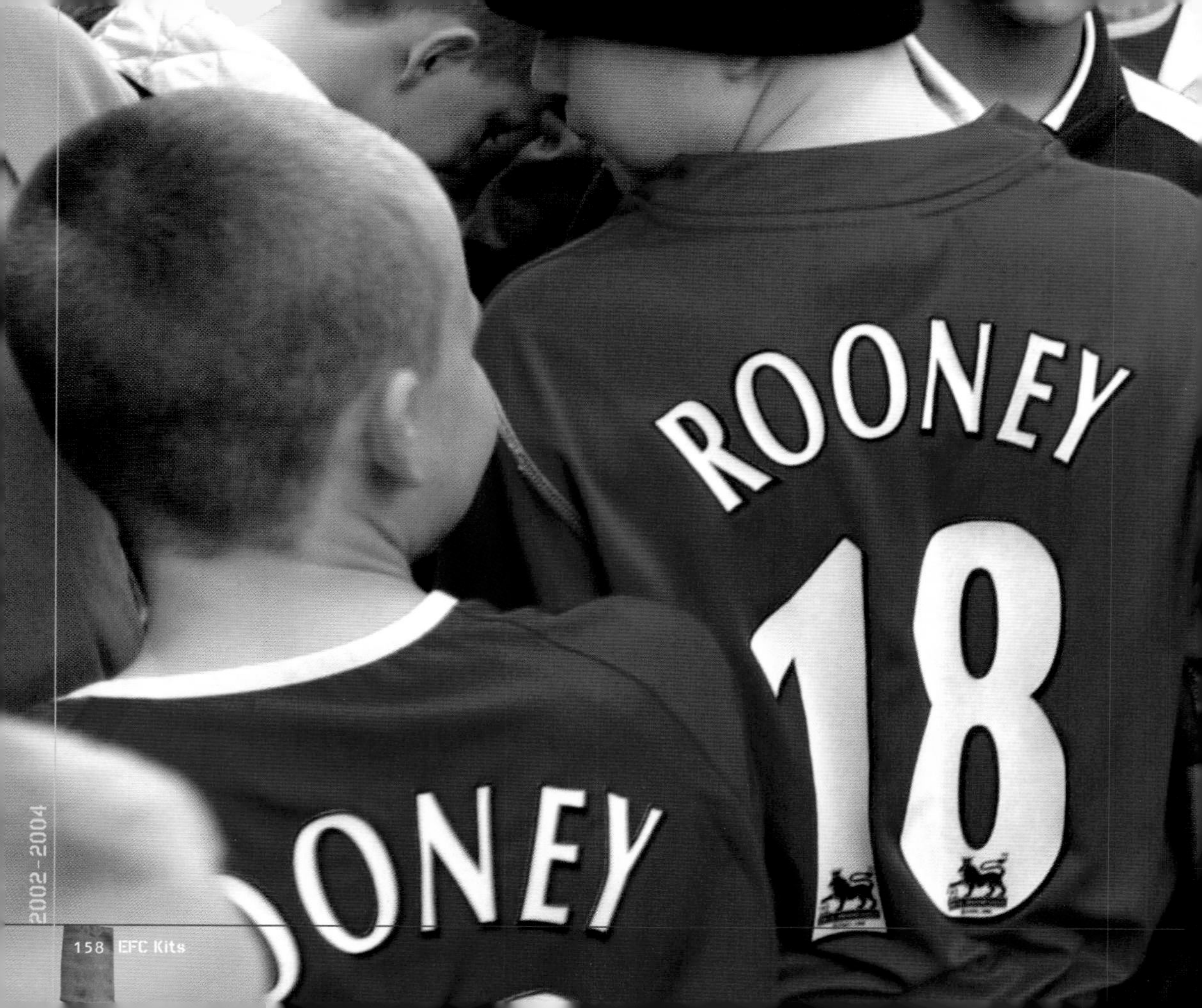
ROONEY
18
ONEY

2002-2004
A kid called Wayne

2002-2004

ABOUT THE KIT

The 2002/03 kit was an Everton rarity — being officially noted as a 'streamlined' strip. The design was the result of feedback from players, who'd suggested that the baggier shirt was easier for opposing defenders to grab. Tighter shirts were beginning to become the norm, with Italian side Lazio's version cited as an inspiration. The resulting top also incorporated stitch patterns, deliberately contoured to show off a players' physique (although not too useful for certain fans). Incidentally, the tight look is officially known as "international fit".

Other innovations included 'USP fabric', designed to transfer perspiration away from the skin more quickly. The white shorts also incorporated the players' number, a trend which had begun at the end of the 99-00 strip. The 2003-04 kit, incorporating labels celebrating the club's 125th anniversary, was a deeper royal blue, which while retaining the round neck, also included white piping. Baggier but still light, there was little variation in shorts — now without number again — while the socks included white piping. There were four more away strips — a simple white with blue or white shorts, and an all black effort in 02-03; and yellow with blue or yellow shorts, plus a rarely seen sky blue creation in 03-04.

2002-03 Home

2002-03 Original home

Everton

2003-04 Original home

ON-FIELD

Everton's best season for seven years, 2002-03 saw the club just miss out on a UEFA Cup spot by a point, a run of only one win and four defeats in the last five games proving costly. The emergence of Wayne Rooney and some shrewd signings were keys to the improvement, with six successive wins, five of them by one goal to nil, enjoyed before Christmas. The Blues were on the end of one of the biggest shocks in recent FA Cup history though. Shrewsbury Town, managed by Everton's most successful captain, Kevin Ratcliffe, knocked the club out 2-1 in the third round. The Shrews would finish the season bottom of Division Three — relegated to the Conference. From the optimism of that season, the Blues flattered to deceive in 2003-04, winning only one away game as they finished a dismal 17th — one place above the drop zone. Their Premier League status had been secured before the final day, more by other teams' ineptitude than an upturn in form. Two draws and

2002-03 Away

2002-03 Away (No sponsor)

four defeats — the final one, a 5-1 embarrassment at Manchester City — was Everton's record for the last six games. Fourth-round exits came in both domestic cup competitions while Wayne Rooney — in what would prove to be his final season with his boyhood favourites — would finish as top scorer, with nine goals.

2003-04 Original away

OFF-FIELD

The 2002-03 home strip was released to celebrate 100 years of top-flight football — Everton being the first club in England to pass this landmark. The 2003-04 season average crowd of 38,943 is the club's largest in the Premier League era — and biggest since the 1977-78 campaign.

FAMOUS MATCH
Everton 2-1 Arsenal
(Premier League).

NUMBERS, LETTERS

Home and away designs for 2002-03 — with Brazilian forward Rodrigo requesting the extra 'l'. His brief Blues career would be cut short by injury.

KIT LOGOS

Both home shirts during these two seasons celebrated landmarks for the club — although the top flight football achievement was more prominent on the shirt, utilising an official crest designed by the club.

DID YOU KNOW?

Wayne Rooney's late winner against Arsenal in 2002 — his first Premier League goal — ended the Gunners' 30-match unbeaten run.
Everton's penalty shoot-out triumph at Newcastle in the League Cup in November 2002 was the club's first success via that method since 1970.
David Unsworth made the last of his record 302 Premier League appearances for the club in 2004.

2002-2004

2002-03 Keeper

2002-03 Third

KITS & KITTEN

The 2002-03 home strip was modelled by Everton supporter and one third of local girl group Atomic Kitten, Liz McClarnon. The idea was that the lines would look most impressive on a lady, a more striking image than on an athletic male.

Other notes regarding kits show Steve Simonsen (left) sporting the 2002-03 black change strip at Manchester City. The keeper was forced to don the strip due to a clash with the goalkeeping colours available to him — namely the sky blue shirt (below, centre), the same colour as City's home strip.

2003-04 Kits launch

2003-04 Keeper

2003-04 Keeper

2004-2005
Unlikely contenders

2004-05

04-05 PLAYERS Thomas Gravesen, Tim Cahill, Marcus Bent
MANAGER David Moyes

ABOUT THE KIT

It was a first for the strip — not only was the kit produced by a new manufacturer, but a new shirt sponsor was also displayed at the same time. Umbro returned after a four-year absence, while Thailand's biggest brewer, Chang Beer, struck up an agreement. The strips were minimalist, with a widened V-neck and white piping on the arms. The 21st century Umbro logo was now without text, the club crest featured a blue, rather than white background and the shirt sponsor appeared more prominent on the shirts. White shorts and socks remained, with the socks featuring a blue band on the turn-ups. The strip was actually worn in the last home game of 2003-04 (with Kejian still shirt sponsors).

2004-05 Home

The away strip was white, with blue or white shorts and blue socks; and there was also an all black third kit introduced, with blue panelling down the sides of the shirt and shorts. The white shirt featured rare green text on an Everton top — in order to feature the traditional colours of the sponsors' brand. The shirts also incorporated simple V-neck designs, with blue trim (on white shirt) and white trim (on black).

2004-05 Launch (Kejian)

2004-05 Shirt crests

ON-FIELD

After the humbling experience of 03-04, Everton were one of the favourites for the drop — having also lost Wayne Rooney after a superb Euro 2004. That the club would go on to finish a Premier League best fourth, thus earning a place in the 2005-06 UEFA Champions League third qualifying round, was little short of remarkable. Only four league defeats in 2004 was key, as defensive solidity based on a 4-5-1 formation proved effective. Bargain signings Tim Cahill and Marcus Bent slotted in well and Thomas Gravesen produced the best form of his Everton career — prompting Real Madrid to sign him. James Beattie and Mikel Arteta came in, but would prove only peripheral figures. Only three wins came in the last 10 games, which included an embarrassing 7-0 reverse at Arsenal — although of these, a shock April defeat of Man Utd, who had knocked Everton out of the FA Cup, proved enough to hold off Liverpool. It was the first time the club had finished above the Reds since 1987.

2004-05 Original

2004-05 Away

OFF-FIELD

The agreement with Thai beer Chang was worth £1.5m for the season. As part of the deal, the Blues also accepted three young players from Thailand, to train with the club. An initial record fee of £20m was paid by Manchester United for Wayne Rooney at the end of the August transfer deadline.

January saw James Beattie brought in from Southampton for £6m — a club record fee, the biggest paid by the club for over eight years. James Vaughan, age 16 years, 271 days, became the youngest player to play — and score — for Everton, against Crystal Palace in April.

2004-2005

OFFICIAL MARK

A new effort to avoid the production of 'dodgy' replica versions, the club crest hologram was a noticeable addition to the shirt.

BADGE ALTERATION

For 2003-04, white/silver were the main colours. The colour scheme was changed for this season, with yellow bordering — and remained so on the 2008-09 shirt.

DID YOU KNOW?

The 1-0 victory over Manchester United in April was the Blues' first win over the Red Devils since the 1995 FA Cup final.
David Moyes was awarded the League Managers' Association Manager of the Year award for the second time in three years.
Everton achieved qualification for European competition for the first time in a decade.

KEEPER CHANGES

An unusual green/blue hybrid was the usual shirt for the goalkeepers in 04/05. Usually worn with black shorts and socks, the shirt also included black panelling. An all grey alternative was also sported on occasion, usually away from home, the shirt again mirroring the other goalkeeping top in the black panelling design. Shirt sponsor Chang Beer also utilised their logo in green type — as they did on the club's white away shirt.

2004-05 All blue

2004-05 Third

2004-05 Keeper

2004-05 Home Logo

OFFICIAL UMBRO PRODUCT

2004-05 Keeper

2005-2006

2005-06
European hangover

2005-2006

05-06 PLAYERS James Beattie, Phil Neville, Tony Hibbert
MANAGER David Moyes

ABOUT THE KIT

A simple blue round-neck and white side piping were the main features of the home shirt, while shirt sponsors Chang removed the 'Beer' slogan from their logo. White shorts with blue piping and plain white socks made up the kit, while a first for the club was the implementation of a European kit. There was no obvious change except arm logos denoting the tournaments, and that the name and number on the back of the shirt was in silver, rather than white, type.

Grey shirts with black shorts and socks was the official second strip — the shirt including black panel design on sleeves and sides. Yellow and blue was also incorporated into a third kit released in

2005-06 Original

September 2005 — although this strip was never worn competitively, mainly because there was no need to use it, with no clubs wearing blue and grey home shirts. The Chang sponsor was in green type on both of these shirts.

2005-06 Home

2005-06 Europe

ON-FIELD

With expectations raised, the season began with a succession of setbacks. Defeat came in the Champions League qualifier, Villarreal — who went on to reach the semis — winning both legs 2-1. However, the second leg in Spain was deadlocked at 1-1 when Duncan Ferguson saw a header ruled out, which would have levelled the tie. Their clincher came on the break soon after. There was no solace in the UEFA Cup either, as the Blues were stunned 5-1 at Dinamo Bucharest, only managing a 1-0 win at home. By the end of October they were also out of the League Cup, and had recorded only one win in nine league games. A win at Birmingham kick-started things, although 4-0 defeats came against West Brom, Bolton and Aston Villa in the space of seven games. Revenge was gained on Arsenal in January after the 7-0 loss the previous May, in a run of one defeat in 11 league games. Having been knocked out of the FA Cup by Chelsea, they came 11th — having rarely figured in the top half.

2005-06 Away

OFF-FIELD

A three-year extension was confirmed with Chang, worth around £6m — the deal again including more young hopefuls coming to England to train with the club.
One of the club's greatest servants, FA Cup and title-winning skipper Brian Labone, died in April at the age of 66.

2005-06 Third

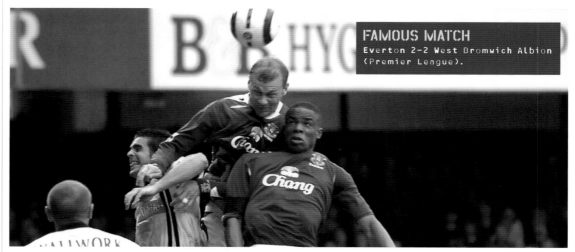

BLUE SOCKS

Change versions, as sported away from Goodison when the home team, whose shirts did not clash with Everton's blue, wore white socks — eg. Fulham.

LIVERPOOL 08

Everton and Liverpool's No 8's were given special dispensation by the Premier League to sport '08' to promote Liverpool as 2008 Capital of Culture for the Merseyside derby at Anfield.

DID YOU KNOW?

Biggest summer signing, Danish defender Per Kroldrup, made only one start after signing from Udinese before joining Fiorentina in January.

Duncan Ferguson's goal in the above game — his only strike of that season — was the last of his career, and a club record 60th in the Premier League.

James Beattie was top scorer with 11 goals.

2005-06 Keeper

2005-06 Keeper change

GREENS & BLACKS

Five goalkeepers were used during the season: Nigel Martyn, Richard Wright, Iain Turner, John Ruddy and Sander Westerveld. First choice Martyn was eventually forced to retire at the end of this season due to a long-standing ankle problem, his final game coming in the FA Cup at Goodison, against Chelsea in January.

An all black or all green affair was the uniform of choice, with the green version being worn generally when a clash with the opposition's kit ensured a change.

2005-06 Back

2005-06 All blue

2005-06 Europe

2006-2007
Back in the top six

2006-2007

KIT DESIGN **Umbro** /// KIT SPONSOR **Chang**

06-07 **PLAYERS** Joleon Lescott, Andy Johnson, Mikel Arteta
MANAGER David Moyes

ABOUT THE KIT

The home shirt changed little, having been unveiled at the end of the previous season — Duncan Ferguson's last professional game. A white retro Umbro diamond pattern was incorporated on one shoulder, while unusually, the Umbro diamond and badge were not symmetrical on the front of the shirt, as had usually been the case. A white and blue round-neck completed the look, the white shorts and socks again minimalist. Blue change shorts and socks were also produced. The collar style was the same on the change kits. The away shirt was white, incorporating sky blue and dark blue flashes on the corners and sides of the shirt — and a sky blue and white collar. Dark blue shorts and socks with sky blue trim

2006-07 Home

completed the kit.
The third strip was in the same style, gold with dark blue touches. The shorts and socks were again dark blue with gold flashes on the shorts and a thin piping design on the turn-ups. Chang type was again green on both shirts, while the Umbro diamond and badge mirrored the home strip design.

2006-07 All blue

ON-FIELD

A bright start to the season set the tone for a successful campaign, which would see the Blues earn UEFA Cup qualification as a result of a sixth-place finish. Eight matches unbeaten in league and cup was an encouraging start, a run that included a 3-0 defeat of Liverpool — while Andy Johnson's Everton career began with five goals in as many games (he would finish as top scorer with 12). Defeat came in a League Cup tie at home to Arsenal, while the Blues were humbled 4-1 by Blackburn in the FA Cup third round. But despite some patchy league results in December and January, and a late defeat at home to European qualification rivals Tottenham in February, form improved with only two defeats coming in the last 11 games. Loan signing Manuel Fernandes proved an inspired recruit while Joleon Lescott, another ever present in his debut season for the club, continued to improve. A 3-0 defeat of Portsmouth in the penultimate game secured European qualification.

2006-07 Third 'dry'

2006-07 Third 'wet'

OFF-FIELD

Forward Andy Johnson completed a club record £8.6m move from Crystal Palace during the summer. Defender Joleon Lescott (from Wolves) and goalkeeper Tim Howard (Manchester United, initially on loan) were other summer signings who would play a big part in the campaign.

Veteran defender and former captain David Weir left the club to join Rangers in January, having spent over seven years with the Blues after signing from Hearts. England World Cup winner and former Everton great Alan Ball passed away in April, age 61.

LEAGUE REQUIREMENTS

The lettering and numbers on shirts are set by the Premier League, and are the same on each teams' shirt. This would be the last season of the Optima Black typeface, apparently squeezed to 60%. The system, introduced in 1993-94 but not made compulsory for another four seasons, gives the league extra commercial exposure.

DID YOU KNOW?

Debutant Anderson Silva da Franca made a two-minute cameo as a substitute against Charlton Athletic in April, equalling the club record for the shortest Everton career.

Gary Naysmith's goal against Portsmouth in May would prove to be his last touch for the club.

Having missed most of 05-06, Lee Carsley played in every league and cup game.

2006-07 Away

2006-07 Keeper change

MAN IN BLACK

Everton's new goalkeeper Tim Howard would usually sport the all black goalkeeping strip, similar to the 05-06 version — with yellow piping on the arms replacing the orange/red tint of that shirt. The design also featured on the change shorts.

A yellow alternative was also produced, mainly worn away from home sporting the 'away shirt' traditional colour of the Chang logo.

2006-07 Home keeper

2006-07 Home keeper (back)

2007-2008
European regulars

2007-2008

07-08 PLAYERS Lee Carsley, Ayegbeni Yakubu, Tim Howard
MANAGER David Moyes

ABOUT THE KIT

A white zig-zag side print, Umbro diamond design on the shoulders and a white, yellow and blue round neck were the main features of the new shirt. The lack of symmetry on the Umbro diagonal and badge remained, while again, there was minimal design on the white shorts and socks.

Another European shirt was unveiled, the legend `Everton' featuring below the players' number on the back of the top. White and dark blue were the away strips, with the Umbro diamonds prominent on the shoulders. The white shirt was worn with dark blue shorts and socks — with a variation featuring additional logos worn in European competition against Fiorentina in Italy.

The dark blue third strip also incorporated white and blue flashes.

2007-08 Original

2007-08 Name & number style

New standardised Premier League lettering and numbers was also introduced on the back of each team's shirts competing in the top flight.

2007-08 Home

ON-FIELD

Boosted by the signings of Phil Jagielka, Steven Pienaar, Leighton Baines and Ayegbeni Yakubu, the Blues enjoyed their best-ever Premier League points haul of 65, finishing fifth – thereby qualifying for European competition for the third time in four seasons. Yakubu would become the first Everton player since Peter Beardsley in 1991-92 to hit 20 goals, finishing with 21. An unbeaten run from the end of October to just before Christmas helped build momentum, while the Blues were unbeaten in the league in 2008 up until mid-March. Any top-four ambitions were hit by injuries to a thin squad. In the cups, a shock FA Cup defeat at home to Oldham Athletic aside, the club's run to the League Cup semi-final was a best since 1988. Eventually Chelsea would run out 3-1 winners on aggregate. An impressive UEFA Cup run also saw the Blues reach the last 16. The run included a group victory over Zenit St Petersberg, who would go on to win the trophy. Having

2007-08 Away (Europe)

2007-08 Third

recorded a European best 6-1 win over SK Brann in the previous round, David Moyes's side went out on penalties to Fiorentina after coming back to level 2-2 on aggregate in a memorable game, which went to extra-time, at Goodison. The eight wins the club recorded in the competition also proved to be the most by any side that season.

OFF-FIELD

Ayegbeni Yakubu signed for a club record £11.25m in August. Everton left their Bellefield training ground, moving into the state-of-the-art Finch Farm complex in the autumn. Joleon Lescott reached double figures for the season, the first Blues defender to score 10 or more for 23 years.

NO LOGO

The club shirt was worn without shirt sponsor against SK Brann in Norway, due to that country's total ban on alcohol advertising.

IN THE PINK

Released to promote awareness for the Breast Cancer Campaign, the limited edition shirts, with money from each top sold going to charity, have been popular with fans.

DID YOU KNOW?

A rebranded Premier League logo featured on the arms of the club's league shirt.
The 7-1 win over Sunderland in November was the club's biggest for 11 years.
Jack Rodwell, age 16 years and 284 days, became the youngest player to represent the club in European competition for 42 years, breaking the previous record held by Jimmy Husband, against AZ Alkmaar.

2007-08 Keeper

2006-08 Keeper change

VARIATIONS

Each European game saw the match marked by text underneath the club badge denoting the 'UEFA Cup', fixture and the date of match. The variables of the 07-08 black and green kits are shown here, with the black including grey and white trim while the green included white and dark green. The other change on these jerseys is the shirt sponsor reverting to white type.

The 2006-07 yellow shirt was also worn at least once during this campaign, presumably due to a colour clash.

2007-08 Keeper (Europe)

2007-08 Keeper change (UEFA)

2007-08 Keeper change

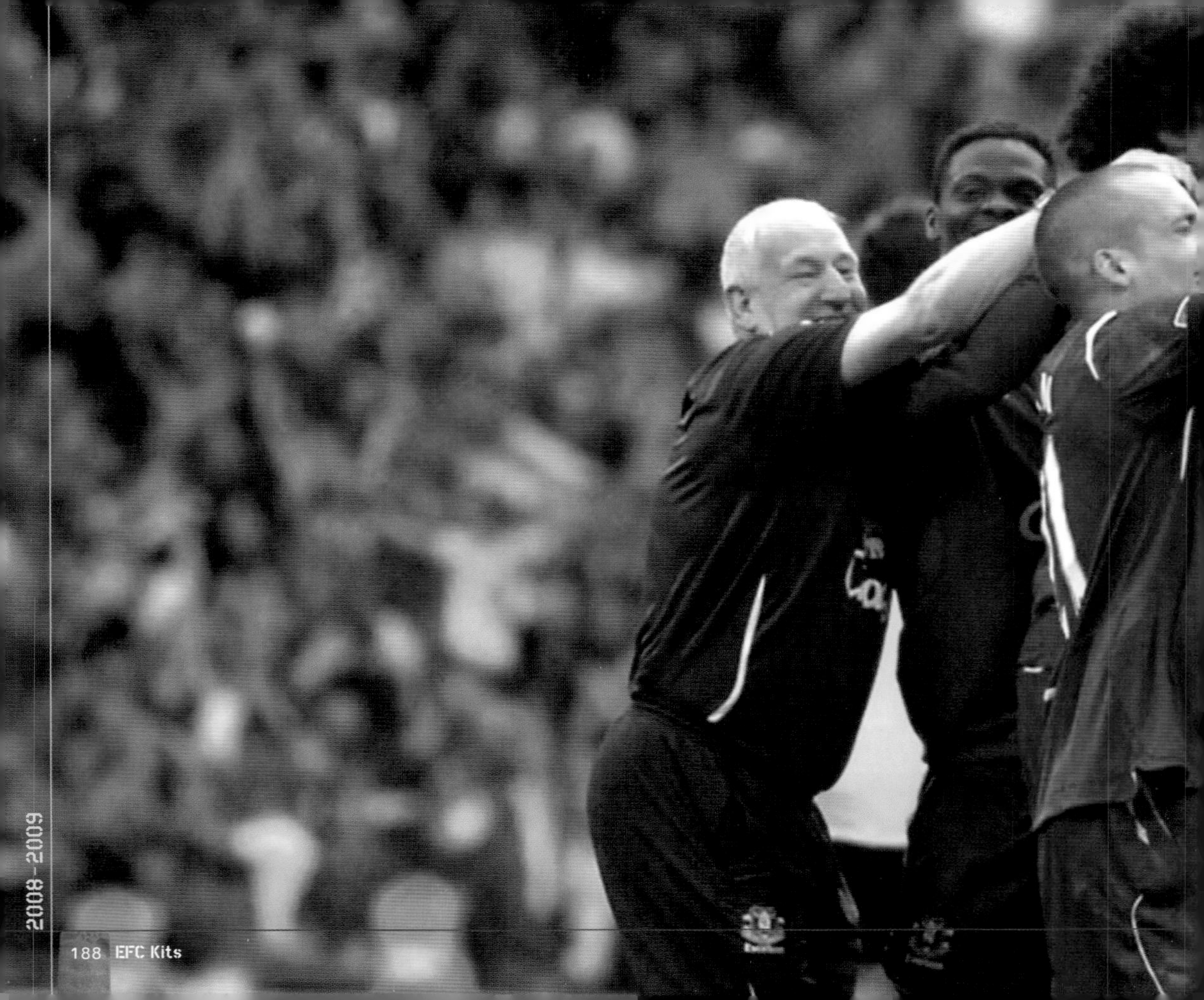

2008-2009
Gone to Wembley - twice

2008-2009

08-09 PLAYERS Phil Jagielka, Marouane Fellaini, Leon Osman
MANAGER David Moyes

ABOUT THE KIT

The last line of Everton Umbro strips maintained the tradition of minimal home shirt changes. It incorporated a white V-neck loose collar, with white piping separating the arms from the main body, and diamond design on the arms. Shorts and socks remained white with blue piping on the shorts, and Umbro diamonds on the socks.

In terms of rules on shirt sponsorship logos, the FA guidelines state that only one single area, not exceeding 200 square cm, be permitted. If the logo is not replicated anywhere else (back of shirt and shorts, and each sock tie-up would be allowed, but half the size) then a 250 square cm logo is allowed. Likewise, a 20 square cm size is permitted for the kit manufacturer — while the club badge cannot exceed 100 square

2008-09 Home

cm, and be used only once on the shirt and shorts. Likewise on each sock — although that too must be half this size. Utilising these guidelines, the white open-necked away shirt also included a grey and black 'hoop' on the upper torso. Black shorts with white trim, and black socks, with white turn-ups plus Umbro diamonds,

2009 FA Cup final

finished off the strip.
A fluorescent yellow third kit was a rarity — the colour was possibly first used in the 50s. Plain with black trim, the black shorts were also similar to the away kit trim, while the socks were also the same design as that strip, with black turn-ups, Umbro diamonds and yellow fluorescent as the main colour.

ON-FIELD

It was a season that began with uncertainty — would David Moyes sign a new deal? Would Everton be able to strengthen a small injury-hit squad? Despite players being brought in at the close of the summer transfer window, the Blues won only two of their first 12 games — including exits to Blackburn in the League Cup and Standard Liege in the UEFA Cup. It took a 1-1 draw with Manchester United and a late win at Bolton — both goals being scored by Marouane Fellaini — to kick-start matters. Following an agonising defeat to Aston Villa in December, the club lost only once in their next 18, a sequence that saw Macclesfield, Liverpool, Aston Villa and Middlesbrough seen off in the FA Cup. All this without the injured Ayegbeni Yakubu, while Mikel Arteta and Victor Anichebe were ruled out in February. A memorable penalty shoot-out semi-final win over Manchester United set up a final with Chelsea, Everton's first since 1995. By then fifth place had been secured for the second season

2008-09 Away

in a row, and 2009-10 will be Everton's fourth season of European competition in five. Unfortunately, player of the season Phil Jagielka missed out due to injury. The quickest goal in FA Cup final history, after only 25 seconds, by Louis Saha hinted at a fairytale success, but the Londoners came back to secure a 2-1 victory.

OFF-FIELD

Marouane Fellaini became Everton's most expensive player, joining from Standard Liege for up to £15m. He would be named the club's young player of the year. October saw boss David Moyes pen a new five-year contract. He also won the LMA Manager of the Year for a third time.

EUROPEAN TEXT

The club's European kit was denoted not only by UEFA Cup logos on the arms, but also by the players' name being noted in lower case type. Premier League names are upper case.

PATTERNED

The modern shirts allow designers to create a variety of logos, shapes and patterns within the material. The 08-09 shirt was a more 'traditional' lined affair.

DID YOU KNOW?

Shirts for Under-18s were produced without the Chang logo due to FA rules related to alcohol advertising. Jose Baxter, age 16 years and 191 days, became the club's youngest ever first-teamer after coming on as a sub against Blackburn in August. Including penalties in the shoot-out against Manchester United, 12 different players scored in Everton's run to the FA Cup final.

2008-09 Keeper

DIFFERENT SHADES

The 07-08 black version again remained the usual goalkeeping kit of choice, although light green (with grey shorts and socks), and light blue were given airings in 2008-09.

The flourescent third kit raised eyebrows, although it was ironically not seen too often in the Premier League. Regarding away kits, the League actually restricts the number of times a team can wear their change strip per season — on eight occasions — unless clashes dictate otherwise.

2007-09 Keeper

2008-09 Keeper

2008-09 Third

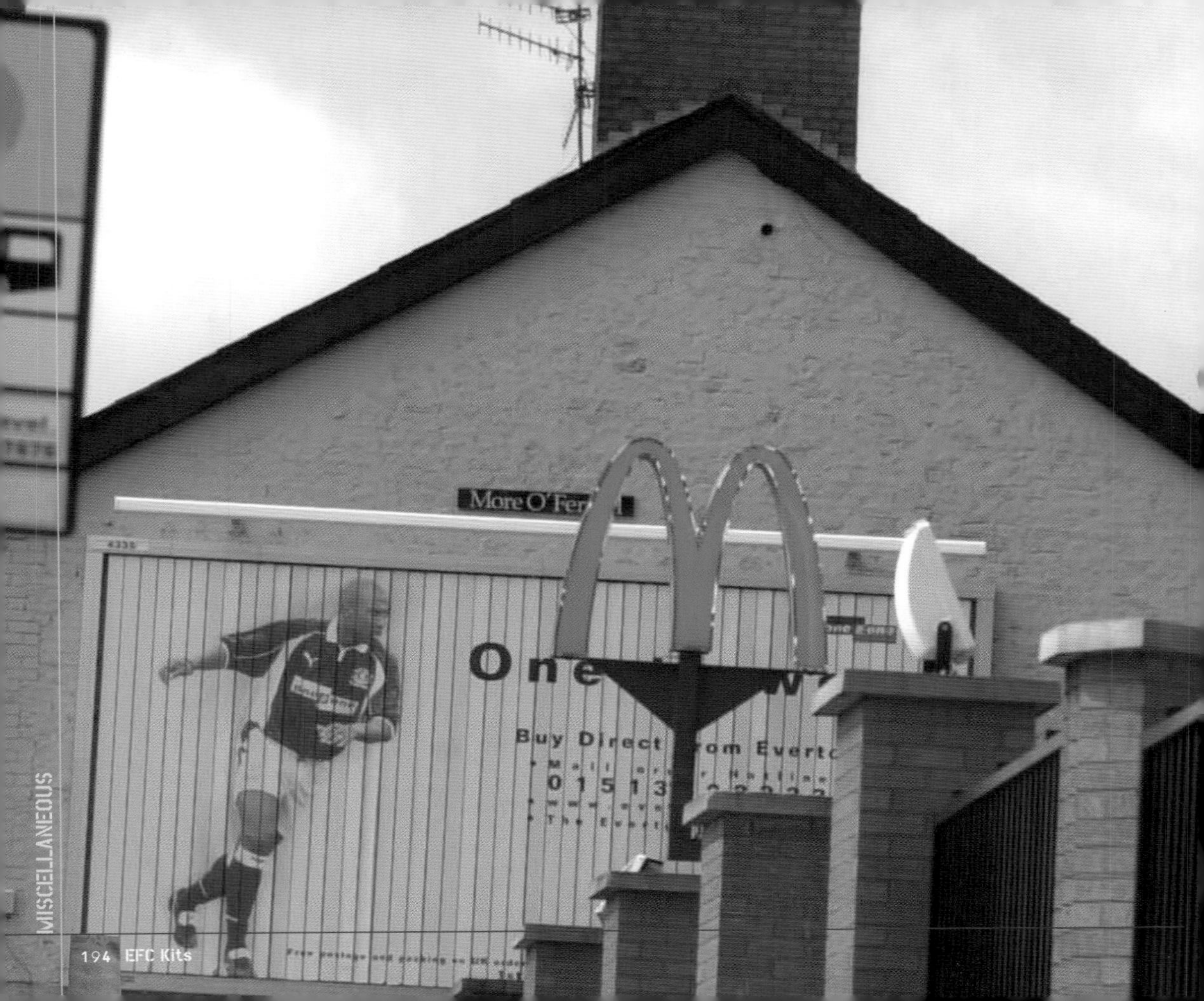
Buy Direct

MISCELLANEOUS
Training kits, manager garb, babies, kit ads...

MANAGERS

1939-1973

Smart and conservative, early Everton bosses were far removed from the 'tracksuit managers' of more modern times. Cliff Britton's trilby is a nice touch, while Ian Buchan opted for the thin jumper addition to his suit. Harry Catterick was said to only slip into a tracksuit when either the TV cameras, or Sir John Moores, visited the Bellefield training HQ – training would usually be left to his coaches.

1948-56 Britton

1958-61 Carey

1939-48 Kelly

1956-58 Buchan

1961-73 Catterick

MANAGERS

1973-1993

From tartan wool to sheepskin, Billy Bingham and Gordon Lee held up the best in 1970s managerial fashion. Howard Kendall Mk I displayed a neat Everton tie, while the tracksuits became more commonplace, with Kendall Mk II resplendent in an Everton shell tracksuit.

1977-81 Lee

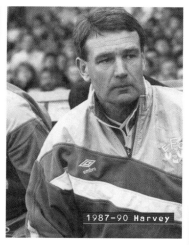

1987-90 Harvey

1973-77 Bingham

1981-87 Kendall

1990-93 Kendall

MISCELLANEOUS

MANAGERS

1994-

Suave and sophisticated, it was a shame that Mike Walker's sartorial confidence couldn't be translated to the players' performances. Everton training and leisurewear was utilised by the club's other managers, with David Moyes rarely seen on the touchline in a suit for normal league games.

1998-02 Smith

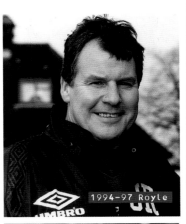

1994-97 Royle

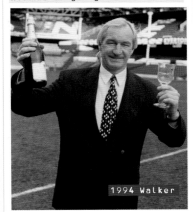

1994 Walker

1997-98 Kendall

2002- Moyes

ORIGINAL KIT LAUNCH

1984 & 1985

A tale in the Everton match programme v Liverpool in September 2006 revealed how Neil Kearns was pictured at the launch of the new kit in 1985. Neil's mother Kathy had written to Le Coq Sportif in March of the previous year having failed to find a kit for her little boy — who was

eight months old at the time. The fact that nobody had asked for a kit so small before was the sportswear manufacturer's response, but they then went about creating a prototype — as the pictures with Adrian Heath show (above and left). When the 'bib kit' was then launched 14 months later, Neil was invited back and presented with the new kit. Kathy recalled: "It's incredible to think he was the first child to ever have an Everton kit like that."

MISCELLANEOUS

TRAINING KIT

1950S-1970S

Woollen fabric and long shorts in the 1950s appeared designed more for the inclement spring conditions. The occasion was actually an Everton training camp down south ahead of the FA Cup semi-final against Bolton Wanderers. The Blues had played at West Ham in the League the Saturday before the game, although in the long run it failed to inspire a

1953 - March

1968 - September

1974 - July

victory as the Trotters set up the 'Matthews final' of 1953 with a 4-3 victory. Lighter training tops and tight shorts were in evidence in the autumn of 1968 (above) at Bellefield. The 'Golden Vision', Alex Young is pictured — he would move across the Irish Sea to take

up a player/coach role with Glentoran soon after. The summer of 1974 (top) and Umbro were now officially providing the training wear, as well as the first-team kits. T-shirts, random player numbers (Bob Latchford in the No 2 shirt) and pumps were a feature of pre-season work.

TRAINING KIT

1980S-2000S

Everton's players leave Bellefield ahead of their journey south for the 1984 FA Cup final against Watford. Traditional leisurewear tracksuits, complete with 'FA CUP FINAL 1984' lettering meant the likes of Neville Southall and reserve keeper Jim Arnold (below left) could travel in comfort. One of his

1984 - May

1994 - January

team-mates would later remark that you could put Southall in a suit, and he'd still look scruffy.
New manager Mike Walker meets some of the squad early in 1994 — pictured are Paul Holmes (above left), and Barry Horne. Light training jumpers were a similar salmon pink to the infamous away

2008 - July

strip still being worn during the 1993-94 campaign. In the first season of squad numbers, at least Holmes sported his — unlike in '74! Fast forward to the Blues' pre-season trip to America in 2008 (above), and as well as light-fabric t-shirts, skipper Phil Neville displays a vest in the humid conditions.

everton ads

WHAT'S OUR NAME: 1983

What to look for in a Hafnia/Everton ad — nifty Everton-related slogan? Check. Andy King resplendent in Hafnia-sponsored home shirt? Check. Seemingly random display of tinned Danish cooked meats? Check. Strangely King appears in the shirt worn between 1979-82, despite it appearing in the programme in '83.

GOOD LUCK: 1979 & 1980

Whether playing Derby County or Liverpool in a Merseyside derby, the club's first shirt sponsors ensured they got the message across in the official club programme. While the earlier advertisement went with a mocked up Everton player in action, the newer version utilised the image of a celebrating Brian Kidd in a non-televised match.

EVERTON ADS

WHETHER YOU'RE CHEERING EVERTON OR BRISTOL CITY...

SHOW YOUR ALLEGIANCE. WEAR THE COLOURS...
OFFICIAL EVERTON AND BRISTOL CITY
SPORTS AND LEISURE WEAR
BY UMBRO INTERNATIONAL

umbro
INTERNATIONAL

DIAMONDS: 1979-80

Umbro made full use of their unique late-1970s kit pattern in the design of their double-page player feature in the official match programme. Here Mick/Mike Lyons reveals how putting a limit on

transfer fees could be a good idea.

The company also celebrated having two opponents on their roster when the Blues met Bristol City in Division One at Goodison. Would the subsequent 0-0 draw have pleased them then?

SOUVENIRS FOR CHRISTMAS

ASA Supporters Jacket 36"-38" only £10.45 | Tee Shirt £2.25 | Hats £1.40 Scarf £1.55 | Everton F.C. Sweaters £6.75 £7.25 | Everton F.C. Sweat Shirt £6.25

All items available from the Souvenir Shop in Goodison Road — Monday to Saturday, 9 a.m. to 5 p.m.

HELLO GIRLS: 1979

Everton players in 'playful' mode, sporting some of the club's wares.

UMBRO SPORTSWEAR
THE CHOICE OF CHAMPIONS

INTRODUCING
MIKE LYONS

MISCELLANEOUS

EVERTON ADS

BIB SALE: 1986

Cheap shorts, cheap socks — shirts almost out of stock (right), and Pat van den Hauwe in action against Oxford United. What price these days an original Le Coq Sportif 'bib' shirt?

GLORY DAYS: 1985

A conversation for the future?'Dad? Dad! Was John Bailey and a toy monkey ever used to help advertise Le Coq Sportif? Well?' The kit manufacturer also went with action shots during the 1984–85 season (right, and above right).

Le Coq Sportif and Everton — a winning combination

GIGANTIC SALE OF EVERTON KIT!

MISCELLANEOUS

EVERTON ADS

UMBRO & NEC: 1986-88
Umbro's link-up with the Blues heralded this rather unusual picture. Home and away strips, plus female in 'leisurewear' is fine — but who's that in the rarely used sponsorless third shirt

Like 91 Football League clubs we're behind Everton.

NEC Corporation. The Computers and Communications Company congratulate Everton FC on a year of great achievement. We hope our partnership will be as successful in the future.

The new sponsors of Everton **NEC** NEC Corporation

(second left)? Meanwhile NEC (above) preferred grandiose statements, revelling in Everton's on-field success as then Division One leaders — and eventual champions at the end of the 1986-87 season.

Professional football at your fingertips.

SUBBUTEO: 1989
Still popular in the late 80s, the tabletop game, which involves an element of speed and skill in flicking the playing figures, was given prominent advertising in the 1989 FA Cup final programme. Unique in offering hundreds of team kits, the Everton figures' shorts even replicated the blue triangle from the home strip — it was just a shame the Blues wore their new kit in that game!

MISCELLANEOUS

EVERTON ADS

LOOK GREAT IN THE LINE-UP.

UMBRO Repli-kit - The Choice of Champions
Step out in style with the authentic product,
made by Umbro the sportswear people - the top
teams choice.
There's no mistaking the real thing - every
garment bears the authentic team badge and
distinctive Umbro diamond trade mark.
Make sure you're wearing the winning kit -
REPLI-KIT.

UMBRO: 1988-91

Everton products on offer
during 1988-89 (above)
included goalkeeper top — the
one pictured wasn't used in
that season — and tracksuit.
Incidentally, the grey and
white away shirt could be
described as a case of false
advertising — the big NEC only

being worn by the players.
By 1989-90 Graeme Sharp was
flanked by two ladies (below)
— presumably he didn't prefer
blonde — with the England and
Scotland kits also offered as
a tempter for fans. For 90-91
(right) models were brought
in to sport the club tracksuit
and home and away strips.

TEAM SPIRIT-
REPLI-KIT.

EVERTON ADS

THE WINNING COMBINATION

THE ONE: 2000

The Blues' first Puma home kit, and what better way to promote the 'product' than with this state-of-the-art advertising hoarding. Kevin Campbell is shown in action wearing the full strip, complete with pun on the club's shirt sponsorship with One2One, and a prime location for Evertonians to glean details of where they could order said strip. Unfortunately the location of this advert was outside the Kop — at Anfield.

Home or away we'll keep you in touch.

 NEC

Personal Computers • Pagers • Printers • Monitors • Facsimiles • Cellular Phones

NEC: 1994-95

Action from the opening day of the season, and the players' face is deemed irrelevent as the copywriter trots out some footballing parlance — home and away, indeed.

PEOPLE: 2006

Chang chose to showcase the club, arguably more than their product in this mid-2000s example. David Moyes' well-documented People's Club monikor for the Blues caught the imagination of the creatives, and thus while Everton were/are the People's Club, Chang must surely be... the People's Beer. Pure genius, as one rival brand may have said.

Other titles produced by Sport Media:

One hundred
years of FA Cup
memories

Celebrating the
more bizarre
Everton games

CD publication
featuring the
Blues' greatest

The best games,
players, heroes
— and more

Fascinating
look at the EFC
Collection

The inside EFC
story behind
the action

Sport Media
A Trinity Mirror Business

All of these titles are available to order by calling 0845 143 0001, or you can buy online and
view current prices at www.merseyshop.com